A Comforting Light

A Comforting Light

Cancer Crusader Mary Jo Cropper
& Her Legacy of Hope

Janice Hisle

Foreword by Dr. Susan Weinberg,
M.D., F.A.C.R.

ORANGE *frazer* PRESS
Wilmington, Ohio

ISBN 978-1949248-241 Softcover
ISBN 978-1949248-265 Hardcover
Copyright©2020 Catherine Chasteen
All Rights Reserved

Proceeds from the sale of this book will benefit
The Mary Jo Cropper Family Center for Breast Care.

Additional donations are graciously accepted by:
The Mary Jo Cropper Family Center for Breast Care
c/o The Bethesda Foundation
10500 Montgomery Road
Cincinnati, Ohio 45242

Thank you for your generous support of this book and of the Center.

Published for the copyright holder by:
Orange Frazer Press
37½ West Main St.
P.O. Box 214
Wilmington, OH 45177

For price and shipping information, call: 937.382.3196
Or visit: www.orangefrazer.com

Book and cover design by:
Kelly Schutte and Orange Frazer Press

Library of Congress Control Number: 2020910093

First Printing

Do small things with great love.

—Unknown

For everyone who is searching for a cure.

—Catherine Chasteen

For Eleanor Ramser, who was my 'Mary Jo.'

—Janice Hisle

Contents

Foreword

This book vividly tells the story of a woman who profoundly affected thousands of lives, including my own. It also tells the story of the medical facility that was founded because of her financial generosity and, just as importantly, because of her personal dedication to a cause. And the story of Mary Jo Cropper also embodies lessons that are important for all of us to learn.

As part of this story unfolded in real time, I played two very different roles. Back in 1995, I was a medical doctor who saw the desperate need for a breast care center. More than a decade later, I became a personal friend of Mary Jo, the extraordinary woman who turned that vision into a reality—and, as a result, left a legacy of hope for the entire Cincinnati region.

The author of this book, who has decades of experience as a journalist, has accurately captured and inspirationally portrayed Mary Jo while also describing the impact that she had on my life, my career, and most importantly, on the community.

Frankly, I was surprised at the extent and depth of the questions that the author posed when she interviewed me. But the resulting chapters were written with such detail and compassion that I found myself reliving the first moments and subsequent years of my relationship with Mary Jo and her entire family. From the time I first met Mary Jo, I marveled at how much her goals and desires were mirror images of my own. We both felt it was so important to treat patients compassionately, not to make them search for care. When a person has cancer, they are already suffering; we shouldn't further impose upon them a fragmented healthcare system. Mary Jo and I agreed on all of that.

The earlier chapters of this book provide a fascinating look into part of the story that happened well before I encountered Mary Jo: her formative years. Dozens of people who knew Mary Jo gave interviews that provided unique insights into her life history and into her personality, a rare blend of elegance and approachability. The author's document-digging and intensive interviewing captured the essence of who Mary Jo was—and produced some anecdotes that surprised even some of Mary Jo's closest relatives.

Mary Jo's childhood and her intriguing family history reveal the backstory, imparting a better understanding of how and why she was perfectly positioned to take the remarkable steps that she did. What a gift—to be able to really have an impact for generations to come! Yet, even though Mary Jo had the financial means to make a gift of a magnitude that few people could, she also did a lot of special things that virtually any person can do. That is one of the important lessons of this book. My friend, Mary Jo, was a teacher by profession. And there is so much we can learn from her and the way she lived.

Mary Jo actually became one of the five most influential people in my life. That was because she taught me what really matters. She taught me not just about family and friends, but about leaving something behind—and how important that was.

Mary Jo's story teaches us a lot about being a true friend, and about being a devoted daughter, mother, wife and grandmother—and a caring human being. It's also a story of hopes and fears, triumphs and challenges, joys and sorrows—the highs and lows that everyone experiences, but that few people can handle with as much grace as my friend Mary Jo did.

I was thrilled when she made her financial commitment and bestowed her family name to our new facility, the Mary Jo Cropper Family Center for Breast Care. For me personally, that was an incredible gift. But it was also an incredible responsibility, because I never wanted to let her down. And when she committed to us, she committed herself and her family to everything we were about.

When she passed away in 2011, I grieved deeply. As I said when I read a eulogy at her memorial service, I do believe that her Center will contribute in some measure to helping find a cure for breast cancer so that future generations of our children and friends will be spared the sorrow we felt when Mary Jo left us— and the sorrow that innumerable other families also have felt when their loved ones passed.

Since her death, Mary Jo's husband, son, daughter, in-laws, nieces and cousins stepped in to meet the Center's every need. We were—and are—a family. Even though I retired from the Center in 2019, I still feel the same closeness, admiration and respect for Mary Jo's family.

As the saying goes, "it takes a village to raise a child," and so it takes a highly motivated team to imagine, fundraise, design, build and run a successful medical facility, such as a breast care center. This reality was captured by the author in her many interviews with employees, financial contributors, healthcare administrators and patients. Her highly personal writing style, punctuated by poignant quotes, allows the reader to experience the emotion and hard work involved in the Cropper Center's creation—and in its evolution as it became part of the new Thomas Comprehensive Care Center.

When I first proposed the Cropper Center, I had imagined a more comprehensive care facility on the Bethesda North campus. Over time—and over many breakfast and dinner meetings with hospital administrators and with my friend, Harold Thomas, who generously funded the Thomas Center—this even bigger dream has now become a reality, too.

I invite you to read about its genesis, to learn about Mary Jo and to ponder the immense impact that one person can make.

—Susan Weinberg, M.D., F.A.C.R.
Past Chair and Medical Director,
Department of Radiology, Bethesda North Hospital/Cincinnati, Ohio
Founder and Past Medical Director,
Mary Jo Cropper Family Center for Breast Care/Cincinnati, Ohio

Introduction

C-A-N-C-E-R.

Those six letters spell one of the most-despised words in the English language; at times, *that word* is still talked about in hushed tones.

And, at first, that was how Ralph J. Stolle and some of his family addressed *that disease*. Ralph abhorred the word, "cancer," so much that he hardly ever uttered it. Yet *that word* left an indelible imprint on him, his business, and his family—especially the youngest of his three daughters, Mary Jo Cropper.

A Kentucky-born inventor and entrepreneur who lived and worked many years in Ohio, Ralph made his fortune in the metalwork industry. In 1962, his company developed machinery to mass-produce aluminum cans with easy-open pull-tabs, revolutionizing the beer and soda-pop industries; in 1983, Ralph obtained a patent for a pop-top opener that stays on the can.

But Ralph also researched human immunity—a pursuit inspired by some of his personal history. In 1928–29, while Ralph was in his mid-20s, he was bedridden with tuberculosis, a life-threatening lung infection that was running rampant then. Two other personal experiences made Ralph acutely aware of the ravages of cancer—even though he avoided admitting it out loud. His paternal grandmother, Anna Mary Stolle, died of cancer in 1934. Ralph's dad, Frank, is listed on her death certificate as an "informant," someone who provided information about her life history. Eighteen years later, in 1952, Frank died of colon cancer. Some people think Frank's family didn't have the heart to tell him that he had cancer. "I guess they thought it didn't do any good to talk about it," Ralph's oldest daughter, Sandy Perry, said.

Rather than just talk about it, Ralph Stolle was determined to take action against *that disease* and others. For decades, much of his work focused on boosting the immune properties of cows' milk on his 3,500-acre farm in Warren County, Ohio. Ralph also partnered with scientists from the University of Alabama and The Ohio State University, obtaining at least twenty U.S. patents related to health and immunity.

Nevertheless, cancer continued taking its toll on members of the Stolle family.

In 1979, Ralph's younger brother, Howard, died in Florida after a bout with cancer, relatives said. (Because of privacy laws in that state, his death certificate was unavailable.)

In 1983, Ralph's wife, Dorothy, died. That was four months after she was diagnosed with aggressive small-cell lung cancer, which blocked a major blood vessel near her heart. A few years earlier, Dorothy "had a spot of cancer on her leg but my dad denied it," daughter Sandy recalled. "Nobody told us about it until later." That cancerous spot was surgically removed. But perhaps doctors "didn't get all of it," Sandy said. She recalls no additional treatment to eradicate stray malignant cells; Sandy wonders whether some of those may have migrated to her mother's lungs, leading to her death.

Nine years later, in 1992, *that disease* struck again. The breast cancer diagnosis of Ralph's daughter, Mary Jo Cropper, strengthened Ralph's resolve to find a cure; he continued to pursue cancer and immunity research even though he was in his late eighties by that time.

But cancer had other plans.

In 1994, Ralph himself was diagnosed with prostate cancer—and *even then,* he avoided saying *that word.* Not even to his closest relatives and associates. At first, he tried to self-medicate by drinking more of the immune milk he had developed. Eventually, Ralph made out-of-state trips for treatment; he kept the details secret. But by then it was too late.

Ralph died in 1996. There was no mention of cancer in his paid obituary notice in the local newspaper, *The Western Star;* nor did it appear in the paper's news article about his death. A story in *The New York Times* stopped short of directly blaming cancer for Ralph's death, reporting only that "he had been afflicted with cancer." But the facts are indisputable on Ralph's death certificate: cancer, indeed, was what killed him—and "extensive" cancerous growths had invaded his bones.

Ralph had gone to his grave believing that resilient Mary Jo had taught *that disease* a thing or two; her cancer had been in remission for several years at that time. But later, her cancer would recur—and, eventually, Ralph's only other children, daughters Sandy Perry and Gail Norris, would both be diagnosed with breast cancer. And so would Sandy's daughter, Cathy Chasteen.

Altogether, based on records and interviews, ten members of the Stolle family have been hit with various forms of cancer, seven of them fatally. All except Ralph's wife, Dorothy, were his blood relatives. Since Ralph's grandmother died, the Stolle family has been averaging one cancer case every eight and a half years. Yet tests so far have failed to establish a genetic link. That might seem surprising. But actually, it's the norm. Despite emphasis on identifying "family history" as a risk factor, the National Cancer Institute says: Inherited genetic mutations "play a major role" in only about 5 percent to 10 percent of all cancers. In other words, *up to 90 percent of cancer patients did <u>not</u> inherit the disease.*

That's why researchers—and families such as the Stolles—are often baffled about the origins of cancer cases. One question the Stolles have asked: Could something about the environment on the family farm be blamed? Doctors have replied: There's no way to know.

The good news about the Stolles' history with cancer: Few were diagnosed while in their prime; most developed the disease in their post-retirement years—and that makes sense, considering that the longer a person lives, the greater the cancer risk, studies have found.

During the early decades of Ralph Stolle's life, most people shared his "never-say-cancer" attitude. Even doctors often kept quiet about cancer. In a 1961 study at a Chicago hospital, 90 percent of doctors said they preferred to withhold cancer diagnoses from patients, as reported in *The Journal of the American Medical Association*. At the time, physicians feared that sharing such news would do more harm than good—contradicting the Hippocratic Oath that most doctors take: "first, do no harm." Doctors routinely engaged in "benevolent deception," hiding the truth because they worried that patients might just give up—or might even become suicidal—upon learning that they had been struck with *that* illness, one that was not only deadly and incurable but was also shrouded in mystery and tainted with stigma. There was an often-unspoken assumption that a cancer patient could be blamed for his or her own malady; perhaps he or she did something to "deserve" it. And that assumption probably helped other people feel as though they were somehow "inoculated" against cancer; they believed that surely *that disease* would never happen to them because they were "different" from "those people," the ones stricken by cancer.

In recent years, research revealed some substances in our environment and some "lifestyle choices," such as tobacco use, can increase a person's chances of getting cancer. Some of the Stolles who got cancer did smoke tobacco, yet some tobacco users in the family died of causes other than cancer. Thus, tobacco use doesn't necessarily guarantee that cancer will show up someday. That's one of the conundrums of cancer: Scientists have yet to figure out why one person gets cancer and another doesn't. "Cancer can happen to anyone," the National Cancer Institute says.

Before research revealed cancer isn't necessarily the patient's "fault," lots of people simply lived in denial of their loved ones' conditions—perhaps partly to avoid the shame that swirled around cancer and partly to indulge in wishful thinking. Ralph's daughter, Sandy Perry, said no one talked about her mother's cancer: "It was like if you didn't say it, it wasn't true."

In the decades since then, the tendency to avoid talking about cancer has diminished; negative attitudes have softened. It's now standard practice for doctors to be up-front with patients, which helps maintain doctor-patient trust and also empowers patients to make decisions about their own care and how to otherwise respond to this life-altering news.

In recent years, TV programs, celebrities and the general public also started talking more openly about cancer. That was especially true of Mary Jo Cropper.

Although Mary Jo inherited many traits and tendencies from her dad, she didn't share his aversion to the word, "cancer." Time after time, Mary Jo would seek out friends, church members and total strangers—anyone she heard was facing any kind of cancer, not just breast cancer—to offer words of encouragement and understanding.

Mary Jo hated public speaking—just as her father did—but she pushed past that lifelong fear and gave speeches to small groups. By sharing her story, Mary Jo educated and inspired others; that's the primary purpose of this book. Mary Jo's loved ones have adopted her mission as their own. Her family now speaks without hesitation about her life, her cancer and her legacy.

Yet many other people still feel uncomfortable, even superstitious, when cancer comes up in conversation. *Brighton Beach Memoirs,* a 1982 Broadway play and 1986 movie, immortalized that phenomenon in its famous "cancer monologue." The lead character describes how *that word* was always spoken softly when relatives talked about an uncle who died from it: "I think they're afraid if they said it out loud, God would say, 'I heard that! You said the dread disease! Just for that, I smite you down with it!'"

Even now, many people seem to harbor a subconscious belief: If we whisper *that word,* the voracious ogre hibernating inside each of us will continue his slumber, undisturbed; we shall be spared his wrath.

That word commands our respect and fills us with fear. Maybe that's because we sense how old and how stubborn this disease has been throughout human history. Descriptions of cancerous tumors—and their incurability—are astoundingly old, dating way back to 3000 B.C.; in 2017, researchers found the world's oldest known case of breast cancer in an Egyptian mummy from about 2000 B.C.

Our reaction to the word, "cancer," is so visceral, it lends credence to psychologist Carl Jung's theory. He believed that we inherit "genetic memories" through our DNA. That appears to hold true with cancer; we seem to innately "know" how much pain, anguish and death this disease has wrought through the ages—for families such as Ralph Stolle's and countless others. Cancer is the second-leading cause of death in the United States, trailing only heart disease.

That word seems all the more disquieting after you consider how it got its name. Under a microscope, a cancerous cell can appear to have "legs" radiating from its center, resembling a crab; the Latin word for crab is "cancer." And, like crabs, these cells seemingly "crawl" throughout our bodies, clustering in groups, clambering over each other and multiplying by the millions.

Faced with such a prolific and intractable enemy, one might be tempted to just surrender. But, as Mary Jo Cropper demonstrated by boldly confronting cancer, there's another choice:

F-I-G-H-T.

Those five letters echo a high school cheerleading chant. But this is no trivial Friday night football game. Cancer thrusts people into a life-or-death struggle—and one of the biggest challenges is this: figuring out how to fight a foe whose many secrets have yet to be unlocked.

As the ancient military treatise, *The Art of War,* puts it: "If you know the enemy and know yourself, you need not fear the result of a hundred battles. If you know yourself but not the enemy, for every victory gained you will also suffer a defeat. If you know neither the enemy nor yourself, you will succumb in every battle."

Like anyone who combats cancer, Mary Jo Cropper learned more about herself—and her fight changed her in unexpected ways, which will be explored throughout this book. Mary Jo also learned about her enemy, seeing firsthand what makes cancer one of man's cleverest adversaries.

Cancer has eluded the smartest scientists' attempts to "know" it. Cancer is uniquely insidious; it finds a way to turn your body's own cells into traitors. Cells must divide to keep you alive. But somehow, cancer shifts that process into overdrive—and the normally life-sustaining process of cell division turns life-threatening. Left unchecked, it eventually becomes life-destroying.

Researchers believe they can eradicate cancer if they solve its greatest mysteries: What causes healthy cells to mutate into malignant ones? What triggers those cells' rampant multiplication? And how can we disentangle healthy cells from cancerous ones?

Even without those answers, modern medicine has learned to exploit some of cancer's weaknesses. If cancer can be discovered before it makes a significant foothold, chances of subduing it—for at least a few years—are very good. With many cancers, including breast cancer, 90 percent of patients live five years or more. The earlier the "stage," the better a patient's chances of survival. As Laura Pulfer, a breast cancer survivor and former *Cincinnati Enquirer* newspaper columnist, once wrote in a breast cancer fundraising flyer: "You can't fight it until you find it." Hence, the push for awareness and early detection.

By the time Mary Jo Cropper discovered the cancer that had invaded her body and her life, the disease had already spread to nearby lymph nodes, small bean-shaped structures in the body's immune system. Aggressive treatment bought Mary Jo some time; she lived nearly twenty years after her diagnosis, about half of them cancer-free.

After tumors and wayward cells have been attacked with scalpels, radiation and medicines, people who have "beaten" cancer may never quite feel "victorious." They must live with the specter of the disease for the rest of their lives.

Like a Gemini, a cancer patient splits into two "selves:" the Normal Me *before* cancer—and the Not-So-Normal Me *after* cancer, the one that endured a treatment gauntlet and emerged permanently altered, from the inside out.

Certain types of cancer carry heavier self-identity baggage than others. Cancers that attack areas related to gender can make a patient feel like "less of a man" or "less of a woman." Such comments often come from people with breast cancer, which makes up about 15 percent of all new cancer cases in the U.S. each year.

Men represent only about 1 percent of breast cancer patients; some didn't even know that men could get breast cancer, and they may feel emasculated for developing a disease that many people associate almost exclusively with women.

For women, a breast cancer diagnosis can be emotion-laden for both personal reasons and societal ones. The female breast is one of the most outwardly visible signs of womanhood. That's one reason why many women feel extra-betrayed by their own bodies if cancer shows up there—and may feel "disfigured" if surgery is needed.

With or without surgery, any battle with cancer usually leaves permanent physical reminders. Radiation and high-powered chemotherapy drugs target cancer cells—but these chemical bombs also inflict "collateral damage" to previously healthy areas of the body, leaving patients to cope with side effects that can surface years later. It's like a cruel, high-stakes version of the arcade game, "whack-a-mole:" as soon as you pound one pest out of sight, up pops another.

Long after the treatments have ended, cancer patients live with daily reminders of their illnesses. Because some foods and other substances have been identified as contributing to cancer, they may constantly wonder: Is it "safe" for me to eat this or drink that? Should I use this household cleaner or that personal-care product? And they must continue taking preventative medicine and getting checkups to ensure that the cancer hasn't returned.

But anyone who has faced the fight probably will tell you that their most valued weapon was an intangible one:

H-O-P-E.

Those four letters spell a small but mighty word, one of the most beloved in the English language and, perhaps, the most potent one in this book.

For hope is what fuels the fight against cancer.

Without hope, researchers wouldn't work to find life-saving and life-extending treatments; patients wouldn't bother to try those new methods; and people would stop making charitable donations to anti-cancer crusades.

All of those efforts have produced measurable progress. From 1991–2015, cancer mortality—deaths from all cancers—dropped 26 percent in the United States. At the same time, the number of cancer survivors increased. In 1971, there were only about 3 million Americans living after a cancer diagnosis; by

2016, that number had ballooned to 15 million. By 2026, the total is projected to reach 20 million.

"Your chances of living with cancer—and living beyond it—are better now than they have ever been before," the National Cancer Institute says.

After a person tests positive for cancer, the first reaction is almost always fear. But after the initial shock, many people feel a surge of hope.

Scientists are studying whether hope helps people's bodies handle cancer. But even if there's no proof that hope can extend cancer patients' *quantity* of life, there's no denying that it boosts *quality* of life for them—and for all the lives they touch.

According to the Merriam-Webster dictionary, "hope" can be defined this way: "to expect with confidence." But that definition seems inadequate when you realize how important it is, especially for anyone facing cancer or other overwhelming adversity. Hope helps us see light when we feel plunged into darkness and despair. Hope can give us comfort when we feel exhausted and overwhelmed.

Mary Jo Cropper understood this. Even when chemotherapy left her feeling weak, she felt empowered when she contacted fellow cancer patients to check on them. For many of those people, *she* was the light of hope; *she* provided comfort.

And, even after hope had dimmed for Mary Jo, she realized: Hope was the legacy that she wanted to leave—for her loved ones and for everyone who comes to the breast care center named after her and her family.

This story will help you learn about that facility and to "know" the woman whose name appears above that doorway.

Even if you never met Mary Jo, you probably will easily picture her being the sort of friend you'd like to have. Although she carried herself with a quiet, fluid grace, there was nothing pretentious about Mary Jo. Her zest for life was infectious. She was a teacher whose compassion for students with learning disabilities flowed freely, as did her love for her family and friends.

You'll be fascinated by her family's history and how it influenced Mary Jo to become a philanthropist—one who gave even more from her heart than she did from her bank account. You'll be touched by her cancer journey. And you'll be intrigued by events that led to the establishment of the Mary Jo Cropper Family Center for Breast Care. That was in 2009—decades after Dr. Susan Weinberg, a radiologist at Bethesda North Hospital, first envisioned everything that she thought a breast center should be:

· large enough to annually perform tens of thousands of mammography exams (low-dose breast X-rays that produce images that doctors check for signs of cancer or any other abnormalities)
· furnished with the latest equipment for diagnosis, treatment and research
· staffed with nurses specially trained to gently guide newly diagnosed, frightened cancer patients along the shortest, smoothest road to recovery
· home to surgeons who specialize in breast care
· a hub where dozens of professionals team up to review individual patients' case histories and make recommendations based on their collective knowledge

After learning about Dr. Weinberg's vision, Mary Jo believed in it so much that she contributed a million dollars to help establish the Center on the Bethesda campus in Montgomery, a Cincinnati suburb.

Mary Jo also gave the place character with her own little flourishes. Mary Jo didn't want a stark, cold, clinical place—like so many of the medical facilities she had visited when she was a patient. She insisted, instead, on making the Center a lovely, warm and inviting place—more like someone's living room than a medical office. The walls and furnishings were decorated in pleasant subdued hues, imparting a sense of comfort; original works of gallery-quality art added colorful accents; plentiful windows filled the Center with light—a comforting light.

But Mary Jo had no idea how brightly the Center's light would shine, spreading her influence long after she was gone—

and touching more people than she ever imagined, maybe even YOU, the person holding this book in your hands.

Mary Jo's story will teach you about her joyful life and about her inspiring legacy, including patient-care improvements that other medical facilities emulated.

You'll learn about confronting cancer out loud, rather than in a whisper—and about fighting cancer, whether it's yours or someone else's.

And, above all, you'll learn more about hope than you ever could from a dictionary.

A Comforting Light

1

Intersections

It was the spring of 1992, and Mary Jo Cropper's life was humming along smoothly—or so it seemed.

Almost a year had passed since she had turned 50, and she felt comfortable in her own skin—a feeling many women embrace after reaching that "fifty-and-fabulous" milestone.

Mary Jo was doing what she loved—tutoring students with learning disabilities. After working more than twenty years for the Centerville schools, near Dayton, Ohio, Mary Jo had been hired in the summer of 1991 to tutor in nearby Lebanon, where she had gone to school as a young girl. By February 1992, the Lebanon school board voted to expand Mary Jo's hours, from half-time to full-time, because there was such demand for her skills.

And, as a relatively new "empty-nester," Mary Jo was preparing to sell the Centerville home where she and her family had lived throughout her tenure with the school district there. Her two children, Amy and Spence, had grown into young adults and were away at college.

Her marriage of nearly twenty-five years was happy and strong; her husband Robert, was using his accounting skills to benefit the company that her dad had founded in 1953. Now, thirty-nine years later, The Ralph J. Stolle Company was still robust. And so was its namesake.

Even though the calendar showed that Ralph Stolle was born in 1904—and had turned 88 years old—the mirror made Ralph appear almost as though he were still a mid-career businessman. He was tanned and healthy-looking in his *de rigueur* "uniform," a dark suit and tie with a crisp white shirt. And he remained ambitious. Having outlived two wives, Ralph now was married to a

Mary Jo Cropper, a few years after she was diagnosed with cancer.

much younger woman who accompanied him as he worked on business deals in Taiwan, Hong Kong and China.

Against that backdrop, Mary Jo and her family had every reason to believe that her lifespan would be as long and as fulfilling as her dad's was; he had already beaten the average American's life expectancy by about sixteen years.

But this spring, something was disquieting Mary Jo. She had noticed a change in the texture of her left breast: dimpling, or indentations.

At the time, Mary Jo had told few people about the anxiety she felt about the abnormality she had noticed. She was very close with her college-age son and daughter, but Mary Jo had told neither of them about her concerns. Mary Jo had a tendency to worry about a lot of things, especially illnesses, but previous fears almost always turned out to be unfounded.

Mary Jo consulted with her doctor, who referred her to Kettering Medical Center near Dayton, Ohio. A surgeon would take a sample of the involved breast tissue, which then would be tested for the presence of cancer. In line with recommendations for women over age 40, Mary Jo had already been getting periodic mammograms—and a couple of those showed suspicious growths that turned out to be benign, her son, Spence, said later.

Now, as Mary Jo headed into surgery, she tried to reassure herself, despite her sense of foreboding: *Maybe it will end up being "nothing" this time, too.*

But troubling thoughts consumed her. Breast cancer was often making headlines then, so it was on people's minds. In the preceding two decades, breast cancer had become a much more high-profile disease in America, thanks to the wives of two U.S. presidents: Betty Ford and Nancy Reagan. Mrs. Ford shattered taboos in 1974 when she publicly disclosed her breast cancer. Mrs. Reagan also gave interviews after breast cancer struck her in 1987. Neither woman died from breast cancer, and both lived more than a quarter-century after having the disease.

Following those two noteworthy cases, breast cancer rates among American women soared. Maybe that was partly because more women were becoming aware of the need to have regular mammographies, and also because detection methods were improving. Regardless of what factors were fueling the trend, the frequency of breast cancer diagnoses made the disease seem to be lurking around every corner. In the years between Mrs. Ford's diagnosis and Mary Jo's, female breast cancer rates had climbed at least 34 percent. And it was particularly prevalent among women ages 40 to 60—years sometimes called "the cancer ages" in 1980s newspaper articles. Mary Jo, approaching age 51, fell right in the middle of that range.

After Mary Jo emerged from surgery, doctors informed her that the tissue was malignant. One by one, Mary Jo's loved ones started getting the bad news about her diagnosis. In 2019, almost three decades later, people closest to Mary Jo still could remember where they were, what they were doing and what feelings they had the day they learned that she had cancer. Each one was able to describe a "flashbulb memory"—a vivid, photograph-like recollection of the circumstances.

Although the precise date didn't stick in their heads, none of them can forget the things that really mattered about that day— and the seismic upheaval it caused.

Mary Jo's sister-in-law, Ginny Kuntz, was sitting in the kitchen of her home near Lebanon, Ohio, when the phone rang. Her brother, Robbie Cropper, Mary Jo's husband, was calling to say that surgeons were removing some abnormal-looking tissue from her left breast. "If it's cancer, they're taking the breast," he told Ginny.

Hearing her brother say the word, "cancer," jolted Ginny. "When you hear that, the hair on your head stands up," she said. "The word is frightening, just frightening."

Ginny made a beeline for the hospital, the same place where she had visited Mary Jo on two happy occasions: the births of Mary Jo's children. Her daughter was born in 1970; her son, in 1972. Now, almost twenty years later, Ginny was filled with dread as she sped toward the hospital. Her heart was racing as fast as her car's engine was.

A horrible sense of déjà vu overtook Ginny. Five years earlier, in 1987, Ginny's sister, Catherine Cropper Trelvik, had died of breast cancer. Catherine was a married mother of one child, a son who was then around age 7—and Catherine was just 40 years old. Ginny was heartbroken. Mary Jo had tried to console Ginny as she sobbed uncontrollably. Ginny kept repeating, "I no longer have a sister."

But Mary Jo sidled up to Ginny and told her: "No, that's not true; *I'm* your sister." Ginny replied, "No, you're my sister-*in-law.*" Then Mary Jo looked her square in the eyes and reiterated her point more insistently: "I am not your sister-*in-law*. I am your *sister.*"

Now, as Ginny made the twenty-mile drive to the Kettering hospital, Mary Jo's sweet words from that trying time echoed in her ears. "Hearing that she considered me her sister, that meant the world to me," Ginny said. And she was terrified of losing her surrogate sister.

At the hospital, Ginny found Robbie in a waiting area. He rose to greet her, but there was no outpouring of emotion; Robbie tended to keep his feelings bottled up. But he couldn't hide the deep worry that his sister sensed. She simply sat next to him, sometimes in silence. Together, they waited to hear the fate of Mary Jo.

Within an hour or so, a doctor appeared and summoned Robbie. He relayed the news to Ginny: Mary Jo's tumor was malignant—and another surgeon would remove her entire left breast late that afternoon.

"I was sitting there in shock," Ginny said.

Then Ginny spotted two familiar faces: Jean Sidebottom and Nancy Sholder. They were fellow members of Lebanon Presbyterian Church, where Ginny, Mary Jo and quite a few of their relatives belonged.

One of those church members, Nancy, was at the hospital because she happened to work there. But the other, Jean, was at the Kettering hospital that day by mistake. She had an appointment at a *different* hospital—but ended up at Kettering because of a misunderstanding, Ginny discovered.

Ginny approached Jean and Nancy, told them about Mary Jo and made a plaintive plea: "I don't know what to say to her. I have no words. Will you come and pray with us?"

Nancy and Jean went with Ginny to Mary Jo's bedside. "Both of them were just prayer warriors," Ginny said. "I just sat there and cried. I was no help at all."

In a sad irony, the women's roles would be reversed in future years. Ginny would be praying for both Jean and Nancy after each of them was diagnosed with breast cancer, too.

Nancy was working her noon-to-8 p.m. shift as a nurse when Ginny asked for help—spiritual, not medical.

"In the tone of her voice, there was urgency, concern, worry," Nancy recalled. "She was intense because her love for Mary Jo was so great."

Nancy, however, didn't know Mary Jo. But Nancy's profession had taught her how to deal with awkward first meetings. "When you walk into a room and you've never met someone before—and they're under stress about what is happening—the calmer you can be, the better," Nancy said. Upon meeting Mary Jo, "I just used my soft voice. And I listened," Nancy said.

After hearing Mary Jo's concerns, Nancy and Jean stood at Mary Jo's bedside and took turns praying with her.

"We prayed for peace and comfort," Nancy recalled, "and for strength to face whatever the future would hold."

Soon after that heartrending meeting at the hospital, Mary Jo mailed a thank-you to Nancy. The ivory notecard, embossed with Mary Jo's initials on front and dated "6/92" at the bottom, reads, in part:

> *Dear Nancy,*
> *Thank you so much for your sweet note. I've thought*
> *of you often and your kindness through "that evening"*
> *and the days that followed.*
> *I'm doing so well. I've completed my first series of*
> *treatments without any side effects....*
> *I've been overwhelmed by the outpouring of love*
> *from family, friends, co-workers and even strangers who*
> *have been through this too....*
> *Nancy, you helped me get through an awful evening.*
> *I will always remember you.*
> *Love, Mary Jo*

Nancy cherished that card. It marked the beginning of a friendship that deepened as it spanned almost two decades. Eventually, Nancy would receive a couple dozen handwritten notes from Mary Jo. "I just thought so highly of her, I hung onto every single one," Nancy said.

Although Mary Jo's cancer saga was just beginning when she wrote that first note to Nancy, one sentence in the middle shows that Mary Jo had already framed the way she would deal with the disease. She wrote: *I feel my life and outlook have changed and I'm not too sure it isn't for the better.*

In the future, Nancy and Mary Jo would be intertwined in poignant situations that neither of them could have ever imagined.

While Mary Jo was undergoing her mastectomy, both of her children were away at college. Neither had any inkling that anything out-of-the-ordinary had happened. Their mother hadn't told them that cancer was suspected.

Because cellphones weren't in common use yet, college students typically would talk to their parents only on occasion, using "land-line" phones—those attached to wires that coursed through buildings. As a result, there was no quick, easy way to alert Mary Jo's son and daughter about their mom's life-changing diagnosis.

Her son, Spence, was in his freshman year at Indiana University in Bloomington, Indiana. He was in his room at the Delta Tau Delta fraternity house when the phone rang. His mom was on the other end. At first, all she said was, "I just had surgery." But then Mary Jo revealed the purpose and the extent of the surgery: removing a cancerous growth *and* her left breast.

"I remember sitting on the floor and just crying," Spence said, "because I had no idea what this meant."

Spence had inherited his warm, engaging personality from his mother. "I'm definitely a 'mama's boy,' and I was very close to my mom," he said, with no qualms about declaring his affection. He couldn't bear the thought of life without her; Mary Jo knew that.

"She kept telling me, 'It's going to be fine,'" Spence said. "She didn't sugar-coat it, but she tried to put a positive spin on it—mostly to protect me, I think." Mary Jo knew that Spence's final exams were approaching, and his college was about 175 miles away from the hospital. Mary Jo urged her son to stay at college for the time being, and to avoid the six-hour round trip to see her. He reluctantly agreed.

Meanwhile, Mary Jo's daughter, Amy, was in her sophomore year at The Ohio State University in Columbus. Amy had just returned to her boarding house, Westminster Hall—one of the buildings where her mother, an OSU alumna, had roomed in the early 1960s. Amy's classes were done for the day, so she decided to call her parents, just to say hello and to check in with them. But Amy was completely unprepared for what happened next. Her dad, Robbie, answered the phone. He cut right to the chase: "Your mom is in the hospital. She has cancer and has had a mastectomy."

Amy was stunned. She didn't know what to say or to do. Her first instinct was to rush to be with her mom. But it was the middle of the week, and rather than having Amy make the seventy-mile road trip now, Robbie thought it would be better for her to come visit that weekend. By then, Mary Jo would be recovering at home. Amy followed her dad's advice but had no idea how she would manage to focus on schoolwork in the intervening days before she would see her mom.

Although Amy's personality was more reserved, like her dad's, she and Mary Jo enjoyed a close mother-daughter bond. As Amy hung up the phone, uncertainty and fear gripped her. "It was such a scary time," Amy said, "because back then, when you heard the word, 'cancer,' that was the same as hearing, 'you're gonna die.'"

"It was like this bomb had dropped and our whole world had changed."

A life-threatening diagnosis such as cancer can give a person a strange relationship with time—kind of like a real-life version of *Quantum Leap*, the science-fiction TV series that was popular at the time of Mary Jo's diagnosis. The show, which ran on NBC from 1989 to 1993, centered around a guy who unwittingly "leapt" through time and space. He would pop up in different cities at various points in history, flitting along a time-space continuum. He desperately longed to return to his normal life, at the precise moment before everything changed. Every cancer patient can relate to that.

In *Quantum Leap*, the past, present and future could commingle; to a certain extent, that also can happen for a cancer patient. When the present is scary and the future seems threatened, it's natural to seek refuge in the past. At times, the past can help us make sense of the present—and sometimes it can provide inspiration for the future.

Mary Jo's future would have uncanny intersections with her father's past.

She was born about a dozen years after her dad, Ralph Stolle, had promised God: If he survived tuberculosis, he would dedicate his life to helping other people.

In the future, Mary Jo also would focus on helping others—especially after cancer threatened to cut her life short.

Blessed with financial resources, Ralph handed out money generously, often secretly. His low-key largesse earned him the nickname, "the quiet philanthropist."

The original Stolle family home in Fort Thomas, Kentucky.

In the future, that description also would fit Mary Jo.

Ralph's most visible act of philanthropy came in 1978, when he and other civic leaders founded the Countryside YMCA, one of the nation's largest YMCAs, on a 126-acre site in Lebanon. Posthumously, the Countryside Y was renamed in Ralph's honor; as of 2019, his relatives were continuing to serve on its board of directors. But during his lifetime, Ralph wouldn't allow the Y to bear his name. He didn't want attention for himself.

In the future, despite Mary Jo's protestations, a building would be named after her, too.

Retracing the past reveals how Mary Jo's future seems to have been preordained.

The Stolle and Cropper surnames are well-known and invoke instant respect around Lebanon, the Warren County seat. There, the Cropper lineage runs deep. The Croppers were descendants of one of Lebanon's founding families. Mary Jo's future father-in-law, Corwin Cropper, and future husband, Robert Corwin Cropper, were both named to pay homage to their renowned ancestor, Thomas Corwin. In the mid-1800s, Thomas Corwin became one of Lebanon's most famous residents. He was a congressman, United States senator, Ohio's governor and U.S. treasury secretary.

In contrast, the Stolle family had no ties to Lebanon—and no claim to fame until Ralph Stolle rose to prominence. He came from a working-class family in Fort Thomas, a northern Kentucky city that overlooks the Ohio River and the Cincinnati skyline. Landlocked on a hillside, Fort Thomas remains a cloistered, close-knit community of about sixteen thousand residents today. When Mary Jo and her sisters lived there six decades ago, the population was about eleven thousand.

Before Mary Jo's oldest sister, Sandy, was born in 1935, their father was already accumulating wealth—a trend that continued as her sister, Gail, arrived in 1937. Mary Jo followed four years after that. Their parents had enough money to purchase a 3,000-square-foot home at 21 Carolina Avenue in Fort Thomas. The house was still standing in 2019, surrounded by other homes. Those didn't exist when Ralph Stolle bought the house. It was situated on seven acres, which Ralph transformed into a parklike setting. Vintage home movies, shot by Ralph, show his three daughters frolicking along paved pathways, past flowerbeds bursting with roses, peonies and dahlias; at night, the grounds would be illuminated by strategically placed lampposts. It was a showplace.

The family was leading a pleasant lifestyle that few people were fortunate enough to enjoy—a fact that the Stolle sisters would not understand until they got older.

But, yes, the Stolle sisters eventually saw that they were affluent—and they knew that was attributable to their dad's drive to succeed. He worked longer hours than just about anyone. Even when their father was not officially working, his mind was a non-stop idea-generator. And he overcame adversity by sheer will, setting an example for his daughters and for other family members who grappled with cancer and other hardships.

Ralph's biography by Ohio writer Geoffrey Williams, *Ingenuity in a Can: The Ralph Stolle Story* (Orange Frazer Press, 2004), is reminiscent of Horatio Alger's classic American rags-to-riches novels of the 1800s. But Alger's remarkable tales were fiction; Ralph's actually happened.

The eldest of six children, Ralph grew up in a family that sometimes was hurting for money. So, he and his brothers would sell eggs, vegetables and rabbits to his Fort Thomas neighbors. Ralph graduated from Highlands High School in 1921, when he was just 17—a year early because he had worked so hard in school. The next year, Ralph launched his own metal-coatings business in the family garage. Soon, Ralph set up shop in Cincinnati. And, in 1927, six years post-graduation, he married Dorothy Judkins, who "literally was the girl next door," Ralph's daughter, Sandy Perry, said. Dorothy was the sole surviving child of a widowed seamstress. By the time Dorothy was 12, her dad had been killed in a railroad accident—which was shortly after both of her brothers had died at young ages. One brother died from tuberculosis; her second brother, weakened from a bout with that illness, is believed to have died from swine flu, Williams' book says.

As a result of this tragic turn of events, mother and daughter were so poor that they could only afford to live in an attic apartment. But Dorothy sensed something special about Ralph, so she pursued him—over her mother's objections. "Her mother swore he would never amount to much," Mary Jo wrote in an email recounting some of her family history in 2010. But Ralph Stolle proved his mother-in-law wrong; Mary Jo wrote: "I'm glad he was able to surprise her."

Dorothy and Ralph's marriage would endure until her death parted them nearly fifty-six years later.

As a newlywed, Ralph led a busy life, running a business and taking engineering classes. But in 1928, tuberculosis threatened to kill him—and, in 1929, the Great Depression jeopardized his business. Ralph clawed his way back to success—and to health. He expanded his enterprises to other Ohio cities, including Dayton and Sidney; in the process, Ralph made smart business deals with big-name corporations ranging from Alcoa aluminum to appliance giants Frigidaire and Whirlpool. Ralph's business acumen and innovations would ensure financial security for his daughters—and for generations to come.

Thus, Mary Jo and her sisters were poised to inherit both mettle and money—two essential elements that enabled Mary Jo to fight cancer and to leave a lasting legacy.

Sisterly love: The two older Stolle sisters, Gail, left, and Sandy, center, dote on newborn Mary Jo in 1941.

For a time, it looked as though Ralph and Dorothy might not be blessed with children. They had been childless for eight years, a situation that Ralph's grandmother, Anna Stolle, lamented. But then Dorothy noticed a problem with her stomach. "Mother thought she had a tumor inside of her—and, instead, it was me," Sandy said, chuckling about the circumstances of her own birth, which Anna didn't live to see. Anna died on September 18, 1934—exactly a year before Sandra Jane Stolle was born.

Gail, as the middle child—two years younger than Sandy and four years older than Mary Jo—was very close emotionally with both of her sisters. Despite the six-year age gap between Sandy and Mary Jo, the two of them had quite a few traits in common. Both grew several inches taller than Gail did. Both were outgoing, independent, fun-loving and a bit ornery; when Mary Jo was only about 4 years old, she would swipe her dad's cigars and mom's cigarettes when her parents were asleep, Sandy recalled. Later, after tobacco use was linked to cancer and other health risks, Ralph Stolle would become adamantly opposed to smoking—and he would become one of Southwest Ohio's first employers to offer smoking-cessation incentives to his workers, longtime Stolle executive Bill Falknor said.

On the day Mary Jo was born, May 30, 1941, Ralph had purchased a tract of land in Oregonia, Ohio, a rural community just outside Lebanon. Ralph called the farm SanMarGale—variations of Sandy, Mary and Gail, strung together, to honor his daughters. But the Stolles would wait a dozen years to relocate to SanMarGale, largely because Ralph didn't want to interrupt the girls' schooling, Sandy said. Stolle insisted that his daughters would go to college—an atypical demand in that era, when young women were prodded to find a nice fella to marry rather than to pursue a career path. "But Daddy understood the importance of education," Sandy said, "so there was never '*if* you go to college'—it was always '*when* you go to college.'"

Before the Stolles moved to SanMarGale, the family continued living in Fort Thomas but would spend some weekends and summers in a small existing farmhouse at SanMarGale. Eventually, Ralph would build a large, modern-looking ranch-style house for his family there.

In the meantime, Ralph's wife, Dorothy, was having problems. Shortly after giving birth to Mary Jo, Dorothy developed phlebitis—vein problems in her legs—and couldn't get out of bed. Dorothy's vein condition would recur over the years, and she would be confined to bed rest at times.

But the Stolle girls and their mother had someone to lighten the load. A cousin on their paternal grandmother's side of the family, Frieda Pirmann, took care of the girls and the house when Dorothy couldn't. "She was supposed to help my mother for six weeks or something like that after I was born, but she stayed for eighteen years," Sandy said, noting that Frieda never married.

Perpetually single women used to be labeled "spinsters" or "old maids," and they were often ridiculed. But Frieda was content in her role. She became particularly close to Mary Jo, acting as "mother" for the first several years of the little girl's life. "Frieda thought Mary Jo was *her* baby," Sandy said, adding that all three Stolle sisters knew Frieda loved them—and they loved her right back, too.

Frieda handled most of the household "business," freeing Dorothy to concentrate on just "being a mom" to her girls, Sandy said. As the daughter of a seamstress, Dorothy delighted in sewing matching outfits for the girls. In one home movie, Sandy and Gail are wearing identical red and white dresses, each topped off with a little red beret, as they cradle their newborn sister outside their Fort Thomas home.

Dorothy taught her girls needleworking and knitting—hobbies that Mary Jo listed among her favorites when she first became a teacher. And, not for a moment did any of the Stolle girls ever doubt their mother's biggest contribution to their lives: her unconditional love.

With Frieda and Dorothy as their main role models, all three Stolle girls learned about compassion and self-sacrifice—traits that would become evident throughout Mary Jo's life, especially after she became ill. Dorothy was particularly good at consoling people and soothing their troubles. She could relate to people's losses and hardships because the deaths of both brothers and her father hit her at such a young age. And Mary Jo said she picked up large doses of those attributes from her mother. In a 2010 email reflecting on her mother, Mary Jo wrote: "Of all three girls, I feel that I am most like her. She was little, like Gail, but most people who knew her think that I am much like her. I consider that quite a compliment."

Frieda and Mary Jo, who were so close emotionally, actually looked like mother and daughter, too. Both were dark-haired and slim. And, Sandy said, compared to many of their bustier female relatives, Frieda and Mary Jo were not so well-endowed. That characteristic led to some good-natured ribbing from family members back in the day—but begged a sincere question after Mary Jo's cancer diagnosis: Wouldn't having less breast tissue decrease the chances of developing that type of cancer? Not necessarily.

Because cancer, as Mary Jo and her family discovered, often defies all logic.

∼

While his girls were growing up—and even afterward—Ralph Stolle segregated his business dealings from his homelife.

As a result, his wife and daughters knew little about his work. When Mary Jo was filling out college paperwork, she even had to ask her mom how to describe her dad's occupation on the enrollment forms.

Their dad was a self-made multimillionaire, but the Stolle girls were oblivious to that fact because of the way he brought them up. They had no exposure to being "rich," "snobby," or "spoiled."

The Stolle sisters never wanted for anything, but their dad taught them work ethic and appreciation for everything they had. As a result, the Stolle sisters were every bit as down-to-earth as their less-affluent friends were.

Like many parents back then, Ralph forced his daughters to join "the clean-plate club." He insisted that they eat all the food they had been served—even the mashed rutabagas that Sandy detested—before he would permit the girls to leave the dinner table. And that rule was enforced "no matter how cold the food got," Sandy recalled. "He was a strict disciplinarian." So was his mother, Kunigunde Pirmann Stolle.

But Ralph's cousin, Frieda Pirmann, released some of the pressure that Ralph put on his girls. When Sandy, Gail and Mary Jo were on summer break from school, their dad would tell them: "You're gonna have your chores," Sandy said, and he would proclaim a lengthy to-do list. But Frieda would intervene. "Then, he would leave the room and Frieda would say, quietly, 'Don't worry about it. I'll do it for you.'" So perhaps the girls didn't end up working as hard as their dad would have liked.

Sometimes, Ralph's demands put him at odds with Sandy. She admits to being strong-willed, as many firstborns are. "I was very domineering," Sandy said, adding with a wry smile: "I got 'accused' of being Gail's mother."

After Mary Jo's sisters Gail and Sandy left home, Mary Jo was the lone remaining child in the household—leaving her to shoulder the full weight of their dad's expectations. That gave Mary Jo new respect for Sandy. Mary Jo told her: "I don't know how you were able to stand this!"

Still, Mary Jo would later commend her dad for being such a kind person, even more so than most people ever understood. She described him this way in a 2010 email: "Hard on the outside but a teddy bear on the inside."

And, even though the girls bristled at their father's heavy-handedness, in the end, the Stolle sisters respected their dad's determination—and that, they learned, is essential for accomplishing anything worthwhile.

Throughout the Stolle sisters' early years, their father was constantly driving to business meetings in Cincinnati, Dayton and Sidney, Ohio—long commutes that infringed on the time he was able to spend with his family in Fort Thomas. In 1953, when the family moved to SanMarGale, Ralph's commute times shortened considerably. Still, Stolle wanted to stop wasting so much time getting from one point to another. That's why Stolle later bought a small private airplane, built a mini airport and installed a runway at SanMarGale.

Although some people might assume that purchasing an airplane is an affectation, that wasn't Ralph's style. There was nothing ostentatious about the way he lived. Ralph dressed nicely but not in a flashy way. In fact, Ralph was so utilitarian that he regularly wore clip-on neckties, a throwback to the days when he had little money. Acquiring possessions was never a priority for him. But he did care about having *experiences*—and he didn't mind paying for them. For Ralph, buying his own plane meant gaining more control over his schedule, more freedom to explore places and more time to spend with family. The latter would become Mary Jo's biggest priority in life—especially after her cancer diagnosis.

By the time the Stolles moved to SanMarGale, Sandy was nearly 18 and was college-bound; Gail was almost 16. But Mary Jo, at age 12, still had one-third of her childhood ahead of her. Frieda didn't make the move to SanMarGale. Instead, she went to take care of her sick relatives in Campbell County, Kentucky.

Life at SanMarGale was an adventure in and of itself, with the airport, a giant lake and another feature that was unusual in those days: an in-ground swimming pool. Mary Jo loved inviting girlfriends to overnight slumber parties and to pool parties that could, at times, be high-spirited. A yearbook inscription reveals that one night, a friend named Bev somehow ended up in the water *with all of her clothes on*—perhaps with a little help from mischievous Mary Jo.

SanMarGale was also home to a menagerie that would have enthralled Doctor Doolittle, the fictional veterinarian and animal communicator. Ordinary farm animals—chickens, horses, cows and dogs—roamed the property alongside an assortment of more exotic creatures: bison, baboons and ostriches. Ralph was funding animal research involving fertility, immunity, cancer and other genetic mysteries. These ventures cost Ralph millions of dollars, but he was truly motivated to benefit humankind—exhibiting a spirit of altruism that his daughters admired. Seeing her dad's unwavering dedication to that goal stuck with Mary Jo; his example gave Mary Jo the right mindset to step up when she learned that funds were needed for the Bethesda North breast center.

Ralph Stolle, a successful businessman, farmer and inventor, taught his daughters about hard work, Christian faith and generosity.

Besides seeing their father's financial generosity, the Stolle sisters also learned about hospitality and warmth from him and their mother. Ralph loved throwing parties for friends, family and business associates—and he would deftly prepare banquet-sized quantities of food, a skill he learned while growing up in a big family. Ralph was best-known for his German potato salad, a throwback to his ethnic roots. His wife, Dorothy, was famous for her sour cream coffeecake. Those two signature dishes became staples at family gatherings, including the Stolle family reunion held at SanMarGale each Fourth of July. That was one of Mary Jo's favorite events of the year because of its emphasis on family, food and fun.

Ralph also cooked for the men and women who worked for him—something that few business executives would ever do. But Ralph never saw that task—or any other one—as "beneath" him; he didn't look down on anyone because he came from humble beginnings himself. Stolle's culinary skills even impressed one of the world's most famous men, astronaut Neil Armstrong. In 1969, Armstrong became the first human to set foot on the moon. He made a statement that has been emblazoned in the American psyche ever since: "That's one small step for man, one giant leap for mankind." Armstrong, who retired to Lebanon after leaving NASA, became a golfing buddy of Ralph Stolle and also became friends with Mary Jo, her sisters and other Stolle relatives. Armstrong helped Stolle establish the Countryside Y, and was known to enjoy Ralph's hasenpfeffer, a dish made with rabbit meat and gravy.

Among the three Stolle sisters, Mary Jo was probably the least-blessed with cooking ability. But that didn't stop her from trying—and improving. And, as time went on, Mary Jo's cooking would become a source of both amusement and endearment for her friends and family.

Amid the hubbub of life at SanMarGale, Ralph and his wife enriched their daughters' lives with Christian teachings—the wellspring from which Mary Jo drew inspiration and strength in her future roles: teacher, wife, mother, grandmother, friend, community leader and, ultimately, cancer crusader.

"We just all had faith; we were just a family that was brought up in the church," said Mary Jo's sister, Gail Norris. "We learned that you go to church every Sunday and you don't miss a Sunday unless something really big got in the way." One of Gail's treasured vestiges of her childhood is a little wooden prayer bench. It occupies a place of honor in her living room in Centerville, Ohio, evocative of the days when she, as a little girl in Fort Thomas, would pretend she was the Sunday school teacher while her sisters acted as her "students."

Religion was always important to Ralph, his daughter, Sandy, said. In his teen years, he had received a pin for achieving perfect attendance at church for five years straight, she recalled. He prayed fervently while he was afflicted with tuberculosis. And even in his later years, when his wife's health was deteriorating, he insisted on at least watching church services on television, Sandy said.

While living in Fort Thomas, Dorothy, Ralph and their daughters attended Christ Evangelical and Reformed Church. Located at 15 South Fort Thomas Avenue, the church is now known as Christ Church United Church of Christ, where many Stolle cousins are still filling the membership rolls, Sandy said.

During 1941–53, when the Stolles summered at SanMarGale, they would attend a small church nearby. Now known as Oregonia-Harveysburg United Methodist Church, the church used to be called United Brethren Church in Christ. A plaque bearing that name remains above the doorway, proclaiming the date it was established, 1873. When the Stolles attended that church, there were only about thirty people in the congregation, Ralph's daughter, Gail, said. She and her family enjoyed the close-knit feel of that group. And the church building itself, at 1444 Race Road in Washington Township, was charming. Like an iconic house of worship adorning a Christmas card, the church had an all-white exterior and long, narrow stained-glass windows.

In the late 1950s, several years after the Stolles began living at SanMarGale year-round, Ralph met people who belonged to Lebanon Presbyterian Church. He gave that church a try—and got hooked. Over the years, Ralph paid for many improvements to the church building, including a new steeple, the bells that peal at service times and the building's first air conditioners, said Ginny Kuntz, Mary Jo's sister-in-law. She suspects that Ralph had a private conversation with the pastor and said something like, "Just let me know if there's anything the church needs, and I'll take care of it." Ginny said no one really kept track of all the donations Ralph made to the church. He preferred to make an impact quietly. "He would come to the church and no one would even know he was there," Ginny said. She can picture Ralph arriving for services. He'd take his customary seat on the left side, about one-quarter of the way from the altar—close enough for him to see and hear the services well, yet far enough back that Ralph blended in with the rest of the congregation. After the service, "he'd get up, smile at everyone and leave," she said.

The Lebanon Presbyterian Church would become one of the most significant places in Mary Jo's life, serving as a "stage" where defining moments would unfold during the next several decades—and even after her death.

Lifelong Relationships

Only about thirty-six miles separate Fort Thomas, Kentucky, and Lebanon, Ohio. But when Mary Jo Stolle relocated with her family from one community to the other, it profoundly altered the course of her life.

Many people are lucky to have one or two close friends, but in the Lebanon schools Mary Jo attracted a busload of buddies who would remain loyal for the rest of her days. Although Mary Jo was shy and a little afraid when she first enrolled in Lebanon, she was fortunate to make friends with schoolmates who were outgoing and included her in their social circles.

One of the first friends Mary Jo made in the Lebanon area was Nan Lesan, later known as Nan Sempsrott. Around the time that she and Mary Jo met, Nan was reeling from the untimely death of her 44-year-old father. He had died in an accident in 1952, the year before Mary Jo moved into the Lebanon school district. After losing the family breadwinner, Nan's mother was thrust into the role of sole provider for Nan and her two brothers. Despite the emotional and economic stress in young Nan's life, her disposition remained sunny—and Mary Jo was drawn to Nan because of it. Nan was known for her outgoing personality. She had a broad, toothy grin that stood out amid a sea of other young faces on a school yearbook page. The two girls' personalities just clicked; their closeness was evident to everyone.

Mary Jo's future sister-in-law, then known as Ginny Cropper, admired the bond that Nan and Mary Jo shared. "They were almost inseparable," Ginny said. "If you saw Nan, you saw Mary Jo."

Like a second mom: Their father's cousin, Frieda Pirmann, left, was devoted to the Stolle sisters: Sandy, Gail and Mary Jo.

In Mary Jo's 1958 Lebanon High School yearbook, when she and Nan were juniors, Nan called her "the best friend a girl could have." As seniors, in the 1959 yearbook, Nan penned a full-page inscription to Mary Jo, expressing fears that the two might go their separate ways, as many people do after high school. "Even if we do make new friends when we leave high school," Nan wrote, "I'll always cherish the true friendship we had together."

But Nan and Mary Jo forged a solid-gold friendship; it never tarnished.

Many years in the future, Nan would unknowingly lay a major steppingstone on Mary Jo's pathway to making her life's most enduring contribution.

During Mary Jo's years at Lebanon, she encountered a handsome athlete, Robert Cropper. Even though each of them would have been considered "a good catch" for the other, they never became high school sweethearts.

The high school yearbook, called *The Trilobite* because fossils of that ancient sea creature were abundant in the Lebanon area, featured Mary Jo as the "Trilobite Queen" in 1959. Her portrait fills a full page in the yearbook. The image is mesmerizing, not only because of the winsome smile on her young, fresh face but also because of her dignified posture and dramatic gown.

Leaning slightly forward, Mary Jo sits with her hands cupped in her lap, palms up—a formal pose that was stylish in 1940s and '50s photographs. She is wearing a classic swing dress, made of taffeta with an organza overskirt and a crinoline petticoat underneath. A sweetheart neckline and shawl collar accentuate her delicate shoulders; the fitted bodice shows off her slender torso. With her short dark hair and big brown eyes, Mary Jo resembles Audrey Hepburn, a Hollywood actress who was popular that year but shot to immortal stardom three years later in the movie *Breakfast at Tiffany's*.

Hepburn also had something in common with Mary Jo besides good looks: graciousness. One of Hepburn's most-often-quoted pieces of advice: "For beautiful eyes, look for the good in others; for beautiful lips, speak only words of kindness; and for poise, walk with the knowledge that you are never alone." That easily could have been Mary Jo's personal motto, based on how she treated others and how she carried herself.

Robbie was a year older than Mary Jo; "He was 'Mister Everything' in high school—good-looking, athletic, popular," his future daughter-in-law, Dana Cropper, said in hindsight. "People liked him. He was everybody's friend."

Although Robbie was less outgoing than Mary Jo, he was involved in a wide range of extracurriculars, listed in the 1957–58 issues of *The Trilobite*. Nicknamed "Crop," he was junior prom king in 1957, the year before he graduated. He also sang in the glee club and belonged to the Spanish club and the yearbook staff. He lettered three years in sports. He played football all four years of high school and was co-captain during his senior year. He played basketball for four years, too. Robbie also played three years of tennis and ran track for a year. Robbie loved physical activity so much, he wanted to become a physical education teacher—an ambition that he later discarded.

Back then, Mary Jo and Robbie's paths rarely crossed. And Mary Jo's girlfriends were urging her to follow her heart and pursue a guy named Warren.

One of Mary Jo's close friends, then known as Joan MacCallum, was smitten with Dick Zecher, who happened to be Robbie's best friend.

Joan's inscription in Mary Jo's 1959 *Trilobite* reads:

> *Mary:*
> *It seems kind of sad to think that we are in our last year of High School together but maybe college would even be more fun. (I doubt.) You are one of my best friends, Stol, and I hope nothing will ever change that (even tho you do get mad when I say, "Drive past Dick's house, Mary.")*
>
> *I sure appreciate you taking me so many places and I hope someday in the very near future you will have someone to drive you around a lot, like maybe Warren. You've got everything to get him hooked, Stolle, I mean that, so now use it. Good luck in everything, Mary. You deserve the best.*
> *Love ya,*
> *Joan*

After high school, Joan and Dick went their separate ways—at least at first. They would eventually marry each other, thanks largely to Mary Jo.

As for Mary Jo and Warren, their relationship apparently wasn't meant to be. Mary Jo never married Warren, despite being engaged to him at one point in the mid-1960s. By then, her heart knew it belonged to someone else: Robbie Cropper.

After high school, fate would draw Mary Jo and Robbie together. Then it would pull them apart, but only briefly, before sending them back into each other's arms for the rest of their lives.

Trilobite Queen

Mary Jo Stolle

Lebanon royalty: Mary Jo Stolle was chosen as a queen at Lebanon High School, where her future husband, Robbie Cropper, was a schoolmate.

Although teens are accustomed to having their own cars now, it was a rarity during Mary Jo's high school years. Mary Jo and her sisters shared a white Ford. And they would take turns chauffeuring their friends around—even though they were embarrassed to drive the car. Their dad had installed aqua-colored panels along the sides to display his experimental aluminum-plating process. "It certainly stood out," said Mary Jo's sister, Sandy.

Mary Jo always seemed willing to share her possessions, to open her home and her heart—qualities that magnetized friends to her, along with her *joie de vivre.*

In many ways, Mary Jo's future took shape like schoolmate Shirley Peyton predicted when she wrote in Mary Jo's yearbook: "Stay as sweet and as much fun as you are now, and you'll always have friends with personalities to match your charming personality."

Mary Jo collected friendships as easily as some women collect shoes; she was at the center of a large circle of girlfriends that remained intact even after some of its members moved away or passed away, said classmate Marilyn Keever Long.

"Mary Jo kept us together," Marilyn said. "She continued these relationships through the years, until the time she died."

The secret to her appeal: "Mary Jo was very witty, outgoing and a good listener—even in high school, she had those qualities that most teenagers don't have," Marilyn said. She described Mary Jo as compassionate. "She always had ears to listen to you," Marilyn said, echoing others' descriptions of Dorothy Stolle, Mary Jo's mother.

A good student, Mary Jo spent three years volunteering with the Big Sisters group, mentoring younger girls. She also taught Bible School during her junior and senior years, which Mary Jo later would describe as the inspiration for her career choice: "Although the time was short, the experience was very worthwhile, for I discovered a great interest in working with young children," she wrote on a job application.

Mary Jo joined Future Teachers of America during her senior year. She would go on to study education at The Ohio State University in Columbus. Because of the university's prominence and proximity—about a seventy-five-minute drive from Lebanon—

many other schoolmates of Mary Jo also chose OSU. So did both of her sisters.

After college, Mary Jo would be employed as a teacher for more than twenty years—even though some people might think she had the financial means to never work a day in her life. But things inside the Stolle family were different than most people might assume, said Mary Jo's niece, Cathy Chasteen. "Grandpa Stolle was generous, but he wouldn't walk up to you and just hand you money; you had to earn it," Cathy said. Still, for special occasions, such as Christmas and birthdays, Ralph Stolle would never skimp. He would give thoughtful, valuable gifts.

When Cathy was in her 20s, she was especially touched that Grandpa Stolle gave her a gold necklace with amethyst stones—her February birthstone—for Christmas. And he gave all the other gals in the family a similar necklace with each one's birthstone. "It showed how thoughtful he was, because it took extra thought for him to find out the right birthstones for all of us," Cathy said. At least a half-dozen female relatives received those gifts, including Mary Jo. Because her birthday was in May, she received an emerald necklace. Mary Jo's sisters, Sandy and Gail, also received the birthstone jewelry. The gals excitedly showed each other the gifts, saying, "Let me see what you got," Cathy said. The following Christmas, the ladies received birthstone bracelets to match the necklaces.

"Among all the gifts Grandpa Stolle ever handed out, those pieces of birthstone jewelry were among the most treasured in the family," Cathy said.

Other than those types of gifts, Ralph Stolle's relatives didn't receive financial benefits just by virtue of being related to him.

When family members needed money, he would put them to work for one of the family's businesses for an hourly wage, Cathy said. As a little girl, Cathy was paid fifty cents an hour to do farm work. She bottle-fed calves and gathered walnuts and hickory nuts.

The patriarch made sure everyone earned his or her pay—a rule that applied even to his closest blood relatives. His daughter, Sandy, supported her family for a while by doing various tasks for her dad, including dropping off complimentary samples of his Stolle immune milk and handing out surveys asking whether people saw benefits from drinking the milk. When Sandy and her sisters were young, their dad would tell them: "Go out there and paint fence posts. I'll pay you a dime for each one you paint."

Thus, the entire Stolle family learned to value work. Later, Mary Jo would discover a type of work that valued *her* as much as she valued it.

At OSU, Mary Jo met a young lady who, like her Lebanon schoolmates, would become a lifelong friend, Martie Bowden, now known as Martie Mehallis.

In 1959–60, Martie's roommate was Marlene Owens, daughter of Jesse Owens, an ex-OSU track star who was world-renowned for his record-breaking performances in the 1936 Olympics. Coincidentally, Mary Jo's father used to tell a "tall tale," jokingly claiming he had run track alongside Jesse Owens; Martie was amused when she learned that bit of Stolle lore during a 2019 interview for this book.

On the same Canfield Hall floor where Martie lived, Mary Jo was rooming with three other girls. Mary Jo and Martie enjoyed each other's company, so they decided to room together. They lived together from 1960–63, in Canfield and Westminster halls, then finally moved into in an apartment at the epicenter of OSU nightlife, High Street.

"Every day in college was a hoot," Martie said. Mary Jo became her very best friend, despite the fact that the two came from family backgrounds that were polar opposites.

Martie grew up in Marion, in southeast Ohio's impoverished Appalachian mountain region. "My family was so poor, even the poor people thought we were poor," Martie quipped.

When she and Mary Jo connected at OSU, nothing about Mary Jo betrayed her upper-echelon economic status. "She never, ever, ever told me anything about her family other than the fact that she had two sisters," Martie said.

Martie was in for an eye-opening experience. One day, not long after the two had become roommates, Mary Jo invited Martie to go visit her family. The two young women hopped into a car, and Mary Jo announced that they were heading to a Columbus-area airfield. Mary Jo had vaguely mentioned something about her dad being a businessman, causing Martie to assume that maybe they were going to pick up a package for him at the airport. "But Mary Jo got out of the car and said, 'C'mon,' and headed toward an airplane that her father had sent to pick us up," Martie said. Dumbstruck, Martie followed Mary Jo's lead and boarded the plane. It was her first flight. "It was a very short hop to Lebanon. Before we knew it, we were touching down on a runway right there on the property, in the apple orchard," Martie said.

By now, Martie was in a zombielike trance—which was about to intensify. "I go into this house and I meet her parents and all. And my eyes are just falling out of my head, because everywhere I turn, I see something I had never seen before," Martie said. Almost six decades later, Martie easily rattled off an array of accoutrements that fascinated her during that first visit to the Stolle household: A tabletop with a built-in Lazy Susan that could be used to spin condiments and food within easy reach of every seat at the table. A water cooler. And an industrial-sized mixer. "It was the biggest mixer I had ever seen in my life—with a giant metal bowl, so big that you could put a bed in there, I think," Martie said. Hyperbole aside, the bowl was about fourteen inches wide and sixteen inches deep, Martie said. Incredulous, she asked, "What do you do with that?" She was told that Ralph Stolle liked to entertain and would use the mixer to make massive mounds of mashed potatoes for his guests.

Martie continued along on what felt like a "Magical Mystery Tour," years before The Beatles recorded that song. "Inside this house, I kept walking and walking and walking, and there were all these bedrooms, each with a bathroom in between. I had never seen such a thing. I had no idea people could live like this…. Then, at the very end of the hallway, there was a bedroom larger than the other ones, with a fireplace in it. And they had unusual doors, like folding doors. I had never seen anything like that, either."

Then Martie spotted the in-ground swimming pool. "I had only seen one other home that had a swimming pool in my whole life at that point," Martie said. "I didn't know what to say or how to make sense of all of this."

Martie wasn't the only one impressed with the Stolle home. Even though it was located in a rather rural area, most people around Lebanon knew exactly where it was, largely because it contrasted dramatically with the rest of Lebanon's housing stock. Established in 1802, Lebanon is known for its farmhouses, historic Victorian-style homes and antique shops. But the Stolle home was truly unique. Ralph Stolle had designed it himself. It was a contemporary ranch-style home with several wings, configured somewhat like the motels that were being built in the 1950s.

Inside, the furniture was unusual, too. Much of it was immovable. Desks and bookshelves were built into the woodwork. A 1974 article in *The Journal-Herald*, a Dayton, Ohio, newspaper, described the home this way: "Its interior walls are horizontally laid slabs of cherry, oak and walnut cut from the farm acres.... From its uniquely placed story-high windows is a view of a large lake and distant Warren County hills. And, to the south, a buffalo herd grazes in spacious meadows."

Amid such jaw-dropping surroundings, the Stolles were able to make Martie and other visitors feel comfortable. Mary Jo and all of the Stolles instinctively knew how to set people at ease, Martie said: "When they were speaking with you, they had a way of making you feel like you were the most important person in the world." They looked you in the eyes. They listened. They nodded. They asked questions about you.

But seeing Mary Jo's comparatively fancy home environment didn't change how Martie felt about her—except she respected Mary Jo even more for displaying such warmth to everyone, no matter how rich or how poor.

"I mean here was this girl, my friend who was just so down-to-earth, and nothing she ever did or said gave me any idea whatsoever that she actually was a girl who had *everything*—and here I was, a girl who had *nothing*, and she was my friend," Martie said. "That just blew me away."

After that initial meeting, Mary Jo's friendship with Martie deepened for a simple reason, Martie said: "She accepted me the way I was, and I accepted her the way she was. It was like she had these things, but they didn't mean that much to her; they were just 'there.'"

However, Martie found out that Mary Jo's unusual upbringing did produce a quirk or two.

Because both Stolle parents were accomplished cooks, their daughters had *zero* experience in the kitchen—an almost unheard-of situation for girls in the 1950s and '60s. Back then, gender roles were rigid; boys were groomed to become breadwinners and girls were taught homemaking skills. But not the Stolle girls. "We didn't even know how to boil water—seriously," said Mary Jo's sister, Sandy.

Martie witnessed that shortcoming firsthand during a subsequent visit to SanMarGale. She and Mary Jo were hungry. So, Mary Jo pulled out a box of frozen Lima beans to heat and eat. Martie was aghast when she watched Mary Jo's preparation technique: "The package said, 'Cook in a cup of salted water.' So Mary Jo put in a little bit of water—*and a whole cupful of salt*—and she thought she was doing just fine, because that's what the directions on the box said."

Martie intervened, exclaiming, "Mary Jo, you can't do that!" Then the young ladies rinsed off the seriously salty Lima beans and started over.

Mary Jo never lived down this culinary blunder. For years to come, the mere mention of "Lima beans" would cause Martie and Mary Jo to erupt with giggles.

Even so, Mary Jo never shied away from Lima beans. In fact, her son, Spence, admitted with a groan: She cooked them way more often than he would have preferred—symbolizing, in a small way, two of Mary Jo's most endearing traits: Her refusal to easily give up on anything. And her ability to laugh at herself.

A postscript: "Mary Jo did end up becoming a pretty decent cook, but she used a lot of her dad's recipes," Martie said. "She was very proud of herself when she did cook something good."

Martie can still envision Mary Jo driving the white Ford Fairlane that her father had given to her as a high school graduation gift—and Martie was stunned to see her soft-spoken friend transform into an adrenalin junkie when she climbed behind the wheel. "Mary Jo was a very fast driver—I'm talkin' *fast!* I just gritted my teeth and held on," Martie said. "She scared me to pieces!"

Once, Mary Jo and Martie had hopped into the Ford and had taken a little road trip. While they were gone, a fire started in their dormitory building, Canfield Hall. When the pair returned, they learned about the fire. "We were so excited because we thought we might not have classes the next day," Martie said. "But then we were shocked to find out that the fire had started in *our room.*" The cause, Martie says: One of the maids, who routinely took care of the dorms in those days, had plugged in a popcorn popper. The appliance short-circuited and ignited. By the way, classes went on as scheduled, much to the young women's disappointment.

Another of Martie's favorite OSU stories: She and Mary Jo were addicted to the soap opera, *As the World Turns*, which was so popular that it ran on CBS-TV for almost fifty-four years, from 1956 to 2010. During Martie and Mary Jo's college days in the 1960s, there was no way to record TV shows for later viewing; the shows could only be watched during their scheduled time slots. And for Mary Jo and Martie, the "torrid love affairs" on the show were irresistibly juicy, Martie said. "So, naturally, one of us *had* to be available to watch that every day, and report back to the other one," Martie said.

But obsessing over the soap opera posed a problem for Martie and Mary Jo. The show aired at 12:30 p.m. weekdays, a time slot that conflicted with a course Martie and Mary Jo were taking in OSU's College of Education. The girls' attendance for that class was therefore spotty at best. Martie went to class so rarely, she doubted the professor even knew she was enrolled. And, as Martie recalls, there were a lot of empty seats for his lectures. "Everybody in class thought he was a jerk, and his classes were terribly boring—which is why we probably continued to watch *As the World Turns*," Martie said, laughing.

Martie doesn't know whether the professor knew that she and Mary Jo were skipping his class to watch the TV show; she doesn't even know whether he took attendance. But the professor did notice that Mary Jo's grades were suffering, Martie said. She remembered Mary Jo describing how the professor had scolded her, saying, "You're never going to be a good teacher—why don't you just get out?" His harsh words stung Mary Jo. "That was just devastating to her, because she really, really wanted to be a teacher." After that, Mary Jo sat out for a quarter. She regrouped and returned to her classes with renewed vigor, culminating in her 1963 bachelor's degree in education.

Many years later, Ohio Governor James A. Rhodes named Mary Jo to a state-level education committee. By then, Mary Jo was a well-established, well-respected teacher—and her dad was a friend of Governor Rhodes. When Mary Jo walked into the initial meeting of that committee, she scanned the room—and spotted the professor who had lost faith in her during her OSU days. Just by being on that committee alongside her nemesis, Mary Jo felt vindicated, Martie said, chortling.

While Mary Jo and Martie were attending—and sometimes not attending—classes at Ohio State, Robbie Cropper and his best friend from high school, Dick Zecher, were serving in the United States Army.

Both had attended classes at Ohio University in Athens, about eighty miles southeast of Columbus and Ohio State, for a year after graduating from Lebanon High in 1958. But then both Robbie and Dick were drafted into the Army, Dick said: "We had no choice." From 1940–73, the U.S. Armed Forces conscripted young American men to fill vacancies, not just at wartime but also during peacetime. Dick and Robbie didn't meet criteria for deferment, so both were required to serve the Army from 1959–61. Neither faced combat duty even though the Vietnam War was in progress; both Dick and Robbie were stationed elsewhere.

As it turned out, Robbie's military service was exactly what he needed at the time, Robbie's sister, Ginny Kuntz, said. He had some growing-up to do. During Robbie's first year of college, instead of devoting time to his studies, he had been distracted by hanging out with friends, Ginny said. Robbie's two-year stint in Germany changed him in important ways, she said. He emerged as a wiser, more mature version of himself.

One change in Robbie was particularly ironic, Ginny said. While growing up, Robbie didn't like guns and never wanted to accompany his dad on hunting trips—yet, in the Army, he was honored with a sharpshooter designation for being the best marksman in his division, Ginny said.

By the time Robbie returned to Ohio University, he was ready to buckle down and get serious about his studies.

And, before long, Ginny's sharpshooter brother would make another important decision: To set his sights on romancing a certain special gal.

3

Loving, Learning, Teaching

Sometimes, love comes along at just the right time in two people's lives. And sometimes, it's the right love—but at the wrong time.

That's actually what happened with Robbie and Mary Jo Cropper—and, decades later, with their good friends, Dick Zecher and the former Joan MacCallum.

For Robbie and Mary Jo, events that pushed them together began as Mary Jo graduated from Ohio State in August, 1963. As family lore has it, the pair's mothers, Mary Waggoner Cropper and Dorothy Judkins Stolle, believed that their children, Robbie Cropper and Mary Jo Stolle, might have been made for each other. The two moms made it their mission to get their now-grown children to see it that way, too.

Robbie was always quieter and less expressive than Mary Jo was. Although Mary Jo was more outgoing, she was not overpoweringly so. That's why the pair of moms thought that Robbie and Mary Jo might click as a couple. And their moms were right about that—just not right away.

Because Robbie's time in the military interrupted his college education, he was still working toward his degree at Ohio University in Athens while Mary Jo had already entered the workforce.

In 1963–64, Mary Jo taught third graders in Springboro, about ten miles north of Lebanon. Her salary: $4,600. But the experience was priceless, as Mary Jo described on a job application for the Lebanon schools in February 1964: "Now, as I am halfway through my first year (of teaching), I can actually see the disappointments, anxieties and worries that teaching involves. But most of all, I can see the wonderful reward of a child's growth in knowledge." Mary Jo then started teaching second graders at Lebanon's Louisa Wright elementary school. That's around the time when Robbie and Mary Jo reconnected. Details of their courtship—and how their mothers conspired—have been lost. But clearly something wonderful happened. Because just a couple months later, on July 22, 1964, while Mary Jo was on summer break from teaching, Robbie and Mary Jo got married—on the same date they applied for their marriage license. They both were 23 years old at the time.

It was a marriage that melded together two of Lebanon's best-known families. Both Robbie and Mary Jo had fathers who were very successful. "I used to say that his dad owned half the town—and her dad owned the other half," said Martie Mehallis, Mary Jo's college roommate.

The pastor of Lebanon Presbyterian Church married Robbie and Mary Jo in the church parsonage. Robbie wanted none of the usual trappings of a wedding. In fact, his sister, Ginny Kuntz, said she learned that Mary Jo had carried a small bouquet for the occasion—and when Robbie saw the flowers, he remarked, a bit disapprovingly: "I told you: I didn't want a big wedding." That made Ginny laugh.

Her brother had a lot to learn about married life, she said. "When they were first married, Robbie gave Mary Jo a sweeper or pots and pans—something practical like that. And my mother said to Robbie: 'Son, you can do better than that,'" Ginny said, then deadpanned: "After that, she got jewelry."

The newlyweds made their home in Athens, Ohio, where Robbie was completing his degree at OU. From 1965–67, Mary Jo taught at The Plains Elementary School there.

Apparently, however, Mary Jo and Robbie had difficulty figuring out how to handle being in different phases of their lives, Ginny said. In 1967, the couple divorced; Mary Jo returned to Lebanon and started working as a substitute teacher.

Shortly after that, Warren, the heartthrob who had been referenced in Mary Jo's high school yearbook, re-entered her life—and asked her to marry him.

By that time, Mary Jo's sister, Sandy was married; Sandy's daughter, Cathy Cranmer (now Cathy Chasteen), would have been about 7 years old. Cathy dearly loved Mary Jo. To her, Mary Jo will always be "Auntie Mary." Cathy also remembers referring to Auntie Mary's fiancé as "Uncle Warren." But his presence seemed to be fleeting. Cathy later learned why.

As the family story goes, Mary Jo was engaged to marry Warren. Her mother, Dorothy, was helping Mary Jo sew some curtains for the home where they would live as husband and wife. In the midst of the curtain-sewing, Mary Jo burst into tears and blurted out to her mother: "But I still love Robbie!"

"And that," Cathy said, "was the end of 'Uncle Warren.'"

Mary Jo and Robbie remarried on August 15, 1969. By then, Robbie had graduated from OU.

The same officiant who had married the couple five years earlier, the Reverend J. Taylor McHendry, solemnized their vows at the same church, Lebanon Presbyterian.

But this time, other things were different. There were more traditional wedding touches, including multiple bouquets. Mary Jo's niece, Cathy, then 8 years old, is clutching a cluster of daisies in a group photo taken outside the church. Mary Jo's sisters, Sandy and Gail, are also in the picture, along with Robbie's sister, Ginny, and about a dozen other relatives. Still, there was no flowing wedding gown on Mary Jo; there was no formal tux-

Ralph and Dorothy Stolle, Mary Jo's parents, celebrated their 50th wedding anniversary in 1977.

edo on Robbie. Mary Jo wore a two-piece skirt suit in a powder-blue fabric, possibly a silk dupioni, which is known for its sheen; Robbie wore a dark suit and tie, with a white flower on his lapel. Later, Mary Jo changed into a less-formal skirt suit in her favorite color, sunny yellow, for a reception at SanMarGale. Photos taken there showed off a three-tiered wedding cake with a heart-shaped topper.

Everyone was overjoyed to see Mary Jo and Robbie reunited—for good this time, giving their mothers the satisfaction of seeing their "scheme" succeed. The couple would remain devoted to each other for the rest of their lives.

Many years in the future, Mary Jo would do a little matchmaking of her own, spawning three marriages—including that of her old schoolmates, Dick and Joan.

A year and a day after Mary Jo and Robbie were married—for the second time—they welcomed their daughter, Amy.

Amy's aunt, Ginny, remembers going to Kettering Medical Center near Dayton, Ohio, to see her newborn niece for the first time. She laughs at how overly cautious the new parents, Mary Jo and Robbie, seemed to be about protecting the baby from germs. "We were told, 'We have masks for you to wear,'" Ginny said, chuckling. "Everything was so sterile!"

Two years later, Mary Jo gave birth to their son, Spencer, at the same hospital. That time, she and Robbie were less paranoid about germs; as second-time parents, they now understood a lot more, Ginny said.

On the day that Spence was born in 1972, Robbie and Ginny's dad, Corwin Cropper, happened to be in the same hospital for hip-replacement surgery, a couple floors away from Mary Jo's room. As Ginny recalls, Robbie went to see their dad and proudly announced: "You're a grandfather—and it's a *boy!*" Up until that point, Corwin's grandchildren had all been girls. And even though he loved those granddaughters, females traditionally change their last names to their husbands' surnames. So, without a male heir, the family name would likely evaporate.

Mary Jo was rather amused when she later told Amy about the anticipation that surrounded the birth of Amy's brother, Spencer. The Cropper children's paternal grandmother, Mary Waggoner Cropper, had told all of her friends about Mary Jo's pregnancy. And Grandma Cropper declared: If Mary Jo's baby was a boy, everyone would know about it, "because I'll be driving through downtown Lebanon, honking my horn!" And that, in fact, is what Grandma Cropper did to herald Spencer's birth, Amy said.

As for Grandpa Corwin Cropper, he was pleased to see that the venerated family name would carry on with Spencer Simonton Cropper, whose unusual middle name came from his great-great-grandfather, Leonidas Simonton. Known as "Lon," Simonton had raised Corwin, his grandson, because Corwin's dad died at an early age. When Lon Simonton died in 1940, he left an estate valued at $300,000—then one of the largest estates ever administered in Warren County courts, *The Dayton Daily News* reported at the time.

Simonton, who made his fortune in the grain business, had served as director of Lebanon Citizens National Bank for forty-five years. After that, another relative on the Cropper side of the family, Spencer's great-grandfather, Charles Waggoner, worked his way up from a teller's job to become LCNB chairman. Years later, Robbie Cropper would serve on the LCNB board. Finally, in 2019, a third member of the Cropper family would become chairman of the same bank: Spencer Simonton Cropper.

Spence's mom didn't know anything about banking. But eventually Mary Jo would make one of the wisest investments that her son, the bank chairman, could ever imagine.

While Spence and his sister, Amy, were young, their family lived in Centerville, a Dayton suburb. Robbie and Mary Jo wanted to live in a place where the Stolle and Cropper names weren't quite so well-known, so their children could enjoy a more low-profile upbringing, their son said. Centerville was ideal in that regard. And it was only a twenty-minute drive from Lebanon, where other relatives still lived.

While Robbie worked as an accountant for a tire shop and then for Ralph Stolle, Mary Jo took off about nine years from her teaching job so she could focus completely on her most important roles: wife and mother. And, following her parents' example, Mary Jo made sure that her children had a religious upbringing; the family attended David's United Church of Christ in Kettering.

"She was very invested in our lives," says her daughter, now known as Amy Cropper Winkler. "We were her whole world; her family was just everything to her."

Both Robbie and Mary Jo spent lots of time going to swim meets after they joined Woodhaven Swim Club on Yankee Road, which was within walking distance from their home on Kings Run Road, Centerville. "Dad officiated; he'd fire the starting gun, and mom would be there to cheer us on," Spence recalls. Amy and Spence swam competitively for about a half-dozen years, until the early 1980s.

Throughout their childhoods, Amy and Spence spent much of their summertime at Lake Cumberland, Kentucky, where their parents owned a houseboat. Even after Mary Jo went back to teaching, that job allowed time off during the summer months, enabling the family to make the nearly four-hour drive from Centerville to their Kentucky getaway.

Lake Cumberland has been called "the birthplace of house-boating" in the United States and even "the houseboat capital of the world" in promotional materials. With more than 1,200 miles of shoreline, the lake covers 63,000 acres and is the ninth-largest reservoir in the United States. The Croppers were among millions of people who visited each year.

The Cropper children could stay entertained all summer long with activities: water-skiing, inner-tubing, jet-skiing and speed-boating. There also were more laid-back diversions: swimming, fishing, canoeing, kayaking—and the simple pleasure of basking in the summer sun and appreciating the picturesque landscape dotted with pink rhododendrons, gingko trees, Eastern pines and cypress.

Amy was only about 5 years old in 1975, when the movie *Jaws* made its debut, causing shark-attack paranoia—bordering on panic—to sweep America. *Jaws* was described as "the most terrifying motion picture from the terrifying No. 1 best seller." And its tagline—"you'll never go in the water again"—became reality for many people who, like Amy, couldn't shake memories of the spine-tingling suspense and the gory images of the movie. Even though Lake Cumberland has no sharks, *Jaws* may have contributed to Amy's childhood fear of water-skiing and possibly falling into the water. She only tried that once, she said, laughing. From then on, Amy preferred to just go to the lake and relax with family and friends. She and her family spent time at Lake Cumberland every summer from the time Amy was 8 until she was 21. She loved sunbathing and enjoying the unique camaraderie that bonds houseboat enthusiasts together.

Spence remembers his parents had shared a houseboat with other relatives for a while before buying their own; "the social aspect of the lake" was something that really appealed to their mother, he said. The Croppers' Lake Cumberland friendships were close and long-lasting.

In later years, after Amy and Spence were both grown with children of their own, the family retreat would be transplanted to a new place, Norris Lake in Tennessee. Even though driving to Norris Lake took about an hour longer than the drive to Cumberland did, Mary Jo and her loved ones would find Norris Lake's restorative qualities well worth the trip. It also would become a place where Mary Jo's spirit would remain a powerful presence even after her physical one was long gone.

As a person who thrived on giving to others, Mary Jo especially loved Christmas and all that it symbolizes.

Like clockwork, she'd send out Christmas cards the day after Thanksgiving. The cards she sent almost always depicted a black Scottie dog on the front; inside, Mary Jo often enclosed a photograph of her family and scrawled a personal note.

Mary Jo loved having her children home for Christmas break from school, which coincided with her own break from teaching duties. One special Christmas memory of Amy's: "We went

Mary Jo and Robbie's children, Amy and Spence.

caroling through our neighborhood on a wagon. Us kids had such a fun time with that!"

And for several years, Mary Jo and Robbie would take Spence and Amy to participate in a downtown Dayton tradition: visiting the legendary Rike's department store. Like many who grew up while Rike's was still in business, Amy and Spence waxed nostalgic about the magical atmosphere of the holiday season there.

Rike's was a Dayton institution. Established in 1853, the store moved to Second and Main Streets in 1912 and began exhibiting its renowned Christmas windows in 1945. It was a big-city style store with specialized departments where clerks were experts on their merchandise and offered gracious personal service. Even though Dayton was only about a twenty-minute drive from the Croppers' home in Centerville, Mary Jo and her family rarely made the trip. But when they did, it was a big deal, Spence recalls.

Rike's employees aimed to make shopping feel like an *event*. Especially at Christmastime. Then, the entire store, with nearly a million square feet, was brimming with sparkling lights and holiday decor. The aroma of freshly roasted nuts would waft through the air, mingling with sugary-sweet scents of chocolate and peanut butter fudge at the expansive candy counter.

Amy and Spence both remember their parents handing them about five bucks each, so they could go to a special part of the store all by themselves: A children's-only Christmas shop called "Tike's," a play on words that melded "tykes" (children) with "Rike's," the department store's name. There, store employees— "Santa's helpers"—would help children choose low-cost gifts for their parents. Then, the children would get help wrapping the gifts before their parents returned to pick them up. The children loved this special privilege and the process made them feel so independent and grown-up, Spence said. After he became a parent himself, he understood that his parents, Robbie and Mary Jo, must have appreciated the experience, too. "I have no idea what Mom and Dad did while we were shopping for them," Spence said, acknowledging, "it was probably the most peace and quiet Mom and Dad had all holiday."

Spence was unable to recall a single gift—or "trinket"—that he or Amy bought for their parents, "but I remember they expressed gratitude and seemed to enjoy each one," he said, "as only a parent could."

Outside the store, a life-size Santa and toy-filled sleigh were perched above a ground-level awning—and were led by pairs of reindeer ascending halfway up the nine-story building. Several large windows, normally used to showcase the latest trends in home goods, cosmetics and fashion, were transformed into fairy-tale-like Christmas scenes where animated figures—such as children, teddy bears and elves—sparked the imaginations of adults and children alike. It was a Disney-esque delight.

Sadly, Rike's went out of business after several mergers; the building was destroyed in 1999. But in later years, some of the original Christmas figures were resurrected for annual displays at the Schuster Performing Arts Center, which sits on the former Rike's site.

Besides the pre-Christmas Rike's ritual, Amy and Spence recall Christmas Eves with both sets of their grandparents.

In late afternoon or early evening, Mary Jo and Robbie would take their kids to enjoy hors d'oeuvres, eggnog, and gifts with Grandpa and Grandma Cropper at their home. Known as "The Gables," the white, two-story mansion is perched on a hilltop in view of downtown Lebanon. At that house, Grandma Mary Waggoner Cropper—one of the "plotting" mothers who got Mary Jo and Robbie together—enjoyed experimenting with new ideas for Christmas decorations every year, her daughter, Ginny Kuntz, said. Grandma Cropper particularly enjoyed decorating The Gables' large front door.

Even without holiday decorations, the home is a can't-miss-it sight for passersby. Located at 229 South Broadway Street, The Gables occupies 4,600 square feet. It also features a balcony and distinctive black iron lacework.

Inside, there were sixteen-foot-high ceilings, more than tall enough to accommodate an impressive Christmas tree. Spence remembers that, in the family room, his grandparents had decorations adorned with real candy canes hanging on either side of the entryway, and he loved being able to snatch a candy cane right off the wall and eat it. Another nostalgic treat: "Grandma and Grandpa would have smaller bottles of Coca-Cola, and it was the only time of year we'd grab bottles out of the fridge," Spence said.

Spence also recalls the old-fashioned configuration of the rooms—which played a role in a frightening incident for him one Christmas Eve. The family room was long and narrow, about fifteen feet wide and fifty feet long, and there was no straight shot from there to the other activity hub, the kitchen. So, if someone went into the kitchen, that person would be out of sight—and maybe out of earshot—for people in the family room. Spence, at age 4, had wandered into the kitchen, away from the rest of the family. Amid the Christmas hubbub, his absence went unnoticed for a while. In the kitchen, Spence grabbed a piece of hard candy, a butterscotch disc, unwrapped it and put it in his mouth—and he started choking. He was unable to call out for help. Alone and afraid, he nearly lost consciousness because he couldn't breathe. He tried his best to stumble toward anyone who could help. Finally, a cousin noticed him and started yelling, "Spence is choking! Spence is choking!" His grandparents' housekeeper, Frances, came to the rescue. She knew just what to do, Spence said: "She gave me a whack on the back, and out came the little piece of butterscotch. She saved my life."

After that, other people came running, Spence said, but when they saw that he was able to breathe, the family just went back to enjoying Christmas as usual.

The year after Spence's near-fatal choking, 1977, Grandma Cropper passed away. Nevertheless, for the next two decades,

The Gables remained a focal point for family Christmases and other celebrations, including weddings. And Mary Jo insisted that, when her son and daughter got married in the 1990s, they each would pose for wedding pictures at The Gables.

Besides serving as a striking backdrop for those photos, The Gables was part of the Cropper-Simonton-Corwin family heritage and Warren County history.

Built in 1848 in the Gothic Revival style with multi-paned windows and a steeply pitched roofline, The Gables was believed to be Lebanon's first architect-designed home, the Warren County Historical Society says. The prominent Corwin family built the house. Subsequent owners included the banker, Leonidas Simonton. He raised his grandson, Corwin Cropper, at The Gables after young Corwin's dad died. Simonton bought The Gables in 1906 and owned the home for thirty-four years before his death. Then ownership passed to the Croppers; Robbie and his sister, Ginny Cropper Kuntz, grew up there, along with their sister, Catherine Cropper Trelvik.

After Robbie's father, Corwin Cropper, died in 1998, Robbie and Mary Jo briefly considered moving into The Gables, where Robbie had grown up. But they and other relatives were reluctant to shoulder the responsibilities and costs of updating and maintaining an old, historic home. Besides, even though Mary Jo appreciated the historic significance of the home, "I don't think it was her style," her son, Spence, said. As a result, ownership of the mansion left the Cropper family in 2002. Regardless, memories of special occasions at The Gables will always remain with the family, especially from Christmases.

After visiting The Gables on Christmas Eve, Mary Jo and Robbie would take Amy and Spence to another celebration at Grandpa and Grandma Stolle's home at SanMarGale. Because all of the other relatives lived close by, "we'd always be the last ones to show up at the Stolle house," Spence said.

Everyone would open gifts all at once there, "so it was a little bit more of a wild environment" than at The Gables, Spence said.

One memorable Christmas Eve, while driving back home to Centerville in the dark, Amy and Spence listened with wide-eyed wonder while a radio broadcaster reported Santa had been spotted by "air traffic control," with his sleigh and reindeer in flight.

It seemed so real to both of the Cropper children. "I remember spending most of the drive home looking up in the sky to see if I could spot him," Spence said. Amy added: "I know it's corny, but I really felt like there was a Santa."

Mary Jo couldn't have been more tickled about her children's excitement. She played into the Santa mystique, Amy recalls, admonishing her and Spence: "You'd better behave, because Santa's elves are watching!"

Mary Jo was so devoted to Amy and Spence, her life as a teacher was somewhat of an enigma to them.

"She never really shared stories from work," Spence said. "She was always all-in with us at home."

This was another example of Mary Jo taking after her father, as he, too, had tried to prevent work from encroaching on coveted family time.

When Spencer was about 7 and Amy was about 9, Mary Jo went back to teaching, but only part-time, so she could still be available for her children.

"She was always home when I left for school, and home when I came home from school," Spence said. At times, tasks such as grading papers or making lesson plans did require Mary Jo's attention outside her normal work hours.

Her ability to juggle those responsibilities impressed Mary Jo's sister-in-law, Ginny Kuntz. "I marveled that she could hold a job and be a teacher and still raise a family the way she did," Ginny said.

With her words and actions, Mary Jo always made it clear that her family was her top priority.

In the 1980s, Spence witnessed a prime example of that. Then a middle-schooler, he had gone to the nurse's station because he felt ill. School officials contacted his mother to come pick him up and take him home. When Mary Jo arrived, she encountered the building's principal. She and the principal knew each other, although Mary Jo worked at a different school—and she was shocked when the principal chastised both her and Spence, asserting that they knew he shouldn't have come to school while he was sick, exposing other schoolchildren to his illness. Mary Jo was insulted. She went into full-on mama-bear mode. She lectured the principal right back, telling him that he was making false assumptions. "He wasn't sick when he left home," Mary Jo said, "or I wouldn't have sent him!"

Mary Jo loved teaching and tutoring. She taught for more than two decades, mostly in Centerville, Ohio.

Spence laughs when telling the story now, but at the time he was shocked to see his mom confront the principal that way. "She had always taught us that the teacher—or the principal—was always right," Spence said. "But in this case, she really took him to the woodshed."

The take-away: Even though Mary Jo respected authority, she wouldn't let anyone run roughshod over her—and especially not over her children.

Time and time again, Mary Jo would prove that her love for Amy and Spence was boundless. And she would fight for them until she had no fight left.

Because Mary Jo became so highly respected as an educator, colleagues considered her a role model. But reaching that status didn't come easily.

She had to overcome a trait she inherited from her father: discomfort with public speaking—which is virtually incompatible with being a teacher and lecturing daily.

Around the time of Mary Jo's 1963 college graduation, a student-teaching evaluation described her as "a very pleasant person but exceedingly quiet in class … she was one of the few students who said nothing all quarter." Her shyness around groups was considered a near-disqualifying flaw. When she stood before a classroom of third graders at Columbus' Beaumont Elementary School, Mary Jo seemed to have "a good bit of apprehension about student-teaching" and appeared to be "afraid that she would have trouble controlling the children," the evaluation said.

But Mary Jo did have a few things in her favor. She projected a professional appearance because she was "meticulous" about her grooming and apparel. And she was "responsive to suggestions," was conscientious and "would try hard." The evaluation apparently was written by the same Ohio State professor who had questioned whether Mary Jo was suited to become a teacher.

Mary Jo set out to prove her nemesis wrong, bolstered by another characteristic she had in common with her dad: determination. Mary Jo overcame her fears and completed her education degree with a "B" average despite her cantankerous professor's opposition. She convinced herself that talking in front of a group of children wasn't as bad as addressing an adult audience, and she devoured entire books about teaching.

Mary Jo's efforts produced rapid progress, documented in her employment records. An evaluation from her first teaching job in Springboro, during 1963–64, noted that, like many new teachers, Mary Jo was "unsure of herself" at first. But she quickly improved because of her "eagerness to learn, willingness to cooperate with supervisors, administrators and fellow teachers," the evaluation said, noting that Mary Jo arrived for work early and stayed late.

She left Springboro to work for a couple different school districts while she and Robbie repaired their relationship, remarried each other and relocated, leading her to seek employment with Centerville/Washington Township schools. Mary Jo surely would have smiled if she had known what someone scrawled at the top of her 1968 job-application form: "Former principal says that she has been an outstanding teacher in their system. Hire her if she will accept."

The Centerville Schools did hire her—and from that point forward, Mary Jo received stellar job-performance ratings and glowing commentary, especially after she discovered her niche as a tutor. As a tutor, Mary Jo didn't have to address bunches of students at once. Instead, she could focus on one, two or a few students at a time; that role magnified her strength as a one-on-one communicator. Tutoring also allowed Mary Jo to more directly see each student's progress, which she found gratifying, especially when she helped students overcome learning difficulties.

In 1969, Mary Jo was commended for her "imagination and animation," an evaluator wrote, adding, "her enthusiasm is contagious … there is a good classroom atmosphere, relaxed but purposeful."

From 1970–79, her son and daughter became her "students." Toward the end of that span, Mary Jo attended a teacher-training course at Wright State University, north of Dayton. Then she returned to teaching and tutoring in Centerville.

For the next dozen years, Mary Jo would repeatedly be commended for fine-tuning lessons to meet each student's needs and connecting with their personalities. Mary Jo once wrote that she tried to create excitement about learning while showing "respect for each child's interests, abilities and expressions."

She would tell people that her learning-disabled students were usually very intelligent "but it's like they had a link that was missing"—and it was her job to identify those gaps and find ways to fill them.

"Mary Jo continues to be a totally effective tutor in all respects," a 1986 report said. Her lessons were well-planned and centered around "activities which the students find interesting."

Like a doctor seeking remedies for patients, Mary Jo "prescribed" solutions for her students. Although she knew how to apply the latest techniques to mitigate learning disabilities, Mary Jo found that paying attention to the little things was just about as important.

For a girl who had low self-esteem, Mary Jo devoted extra time and encouragement; for a boy who hated writing down book reports, she offered the option of making voice-recorded versions.

For the disinterested, she provided incentives, such as "poker chips" that could be redeemed for prizes.

For the undisciplined, she drew boundaries. When one boy's silly antics disrupted other students, "she became very firm with him, which had a settling effect," a 1987 report said, demonstrating "she can be firm when she needs to be."

And for everyone, she engendered warmth and comfort in the classroom, just as she did in other areas of her life. In 1988, an observer noted that Mary Jo created "a warm feeling" among her students as she chatted with them at the beginning of their tutoring session. In 1990, when a student was complaining about the room being cold, Mary Jo suggested that he leave on his jacket.

Mary Jo now knew what to do and how to do it.

After a slightly shaky liftoff, Mary Jo was soaring as a teacher—and so were her students. As years passed, Mary Jo would be overjoyed when she heard about each of her former students graduating from college, an achievement that might have been out of reach without her help.

Besides the loving relationships she shared with her schoolchildren and with her own children, Mary Jo also forged close bonds with other relatives, including a niece, Cathy Cranmer Chasteen. Since 1989, Cathy has lived in Warren County's Turtlecreek Township, near the former SanMarGale property where Mary Jo and her sisters grew up.

For Cathy, Mary Jo—or "Auntie Mary"—was almost like a big sister. "When I was pretty little, she was just this 'larger-than-life' person," Cathy said. The same thing was often said about Mary Jo's father, Ralph Stolle, too.

In 1961, when Cathy was born to Mary Jo's oldest sister, Sandy, Mary Jo was 20, and she reminded Cathy of a TV actress who had become America's sweetheart: Mary Tyler Moore. She starred in *The Dick Van Dyke Show* during the 1960s; in the '70s, she headlined *The Mary Tyler Moore Show*.

Mary Jo "sort of looked like her," Cathy said. Both were pretty brown-eyed brunettes. Both were "always 'put-together,'"

Cathy said, with classy wardrobes. Mary Jo's build was also similar to Mary Tyler Moore's. Both stood about five feet, seven inches and were slim; Mary Jo weighed about 120 pounds around the time that Cathy would have first met her. And the actress' on-air persona had the same moxie that Mary Jo did in real life.

Cathy loved Auntie Mary from the start. Probably her earliest memory of Mary Jo was one Thanksgiving, perhaps 1966, when Mary Jo and Robbie's first marriage was imperiled. Relatives had gathered at Grandpa and Grandma Stolle's house at SanMarGale for Thanksgiving dinner, and Mary Jo invited Cathy to come to her apartment in Lebanon to eat chili afterward. Cathy eagerly went, despite what was on the menu. "I just wanted to go spend time with her—but I didn't like chili," she said, laughing. "And, if I recall correctly, I didn't end up eating chili that day, either. I just enjoyed being with Auntie Mary."

To Cathy, Auntie Mary's personality was like the chair that Goldilocks finally found in the fairytale: "just right."

"She wasn't meek and mild, but she wasn't loud, either," Cathy said. "If there was a room with fifteen people in it, by the end of the visit, she would have talked with everybody. People gravitated toward her because she was genuine."

Mary Jo also had a great sense of humor. She and Cathy shared quite a few laughs watching *The Carol Burnett Show,* a comedy and variety show that ran on CBS-TV from 1967–78. Now, more than four decades later, episodes of that show still attract millions of viewers on the internet, via YouTube. So do Mary Tyler Moore's shows.

Cathy loved sharing funny stories with Auntie Mary, who would exclaim, "Ohhh, Cathy!" as she playfully swiped a hand across Cathy's arm.

But Mary Jo also knew when to be serious.

One thing she took seriously was education, especially after that Ohio State education professor came down hard on her. And education was a value that Auntie Mary instilled in Cathy.

Mary Jo was always asking Cathy what was going on in school and what kind of grades she was earning. Mary Jo also rewarded Cathy for school attendance. Mary Jo held a ten-dollar bill in front of Cathy and told her: "If you don't miss another day of school, I'll give you this." Cathy had zero absences for the rest of that year—and Auntie Mary handed over the money.

"She always wanted you to do the best that you could do," Cathy said. "She was very encouraging."

Auntie Mary often helped Cathy with spelling. On one such occasion, Cathy was about 8 years old. She and Mary Jo sat in the back seat of a car while Grandpa and Grandma Stolle sat in front, driving them to church. And Mary Jo helped Cathy spell out the church's name: "P-r-e-s-b-y-t-e-r-i-a-n." To this day, "every time someone asks me how to spell a word, I think of her," Cathy said.

Cathy also remembers Auntie Mary conducting "summer school" for her, her older brother, Curt, and cousin Brad Norris (son of Cathy's Auntie Gail). "We learned how to sit at a table and have proper manners," Cathy said. "We would get gold stars if we did well." Mary Jo would affix the gold-star stickers on a chart for each of her three "students." At the conclusion of the summer, "whoever had the most gold stars would get an ice cream at Dairy Queen or whatever," Cathy said.

Cathy cherishes an education-related gift that Mary Jo gave her when she graduated from Lebanon High School in 1979: a *Webster's New Collegiate Dictionary*. Cathy used to keep it on her nightstand. She remembers consulting that dictionary frequently. Even though electronic versions have supplanted printed dictionaries for most people, Cathy still displays the book on a shelf in her office now, more than forty years after she received it. Copyrighted 1977, the dictionary from Auntie Mary has a reddish-orange cover that has faded; its corners are a bit worn. There's no inscription inside. But none was needed. Because, for Cathy, the book was then—and continues to be—a silent testimonial to Auntie Mary's undying love and concern for her.

To Cathy's surprise, Mary Jo's love and concern for others would help Cathy navigate the scariest time of her life, long after Auntie Mary had been laid to rest.

Charting a New Course

Affter hearing she had cancer, Mary Jo Cropper felt like she had suddenly been plopped into the driver's seat of an unfamiliar vehicle. Careening along a strange path without a road map, Mary Jo and her family would hold on tight for a long, bumpy ride.

But Mary Jo was determined to take control as best she could. She would figure out how to shift gears, which way to turn and how to ease the white-knuckle tension that gripped her and everyone who cared about her.

In the decade or so prior to her diagnosis, Mary Jo had mourned the deaths of three family members, two of whom had cancer.

In June 1983, cancer-related problems claimed the life of her mother, Dorothy, at age 76. Shortly thereafter, Mary Jo and her sisters, Sandy and Gail, paid a visit to Frieda Pirmann, the relative who had helped their mother care for them. Frieda was in ill health at the Lakeside Place nursing home, in Highland Heights, Kentucky. She was 71, five years younger than Dorothy, and had no sign of cancer. Instead, Frieda had suffered for years with rheumatoid arthritis and cardiovascular problems. Mary Jo's sister, Sandy, recalls a poignant moment: While lamenting Dorothy's passing, Frieda said, "It should've been me instead of your mother." Frieda died of heart failure that September, shortly after the Stolle sisters' visit.

A couple years later, Mary Jo's sister-in-law, Catherine Cropper Trelvik, was diagnosed with an aggressive form of breast cancer. Mary Jo and her husband, Robbie, did what they could to help. They would babysit Catherine's young son, Thomas, and also brought meals to Catherine and her husband, Arne. But in

Dad and his girls: Ralph Stolle with his daughters, Sandy, Gail and Mary Jo, enjoyed a visit at his second home in Fort Myers, Florida. Around the time this photo was taken, Mary Jo was diagnosed with cancer.

1987, Catherine passed away at age 40—the third death close to Mary Jo in a four-year timeframe.

That trio of deaths caused Mary Jo, then in her mid-40s, to think more about her own lifespan. Because her mother had developed lung cancer after years of cigarette smoking, Mary Jo decided to quit that habit shortly after her mother died. Later, Mary Jo told her family: "I wish I had never smoked." She believed that smoking may have been a catalyst for her breast cancer.

Although the National Cancer Institute says smoking is believed to have "little or no effect" on breast cancer risk, the institute still advises people to avoid smoking and other suspected risks that are controllable. Thus, a person might be able to partially offset factors that are uncontrollable, such as age, genetics and family health history. Breast cancer does tend to run in families. A person's chances of getting breast cancer may even double if a "first-degree" relative—parent, sibling or child—is diagnosed. There were no such connections for Mary Jo at the time of her diagnosis.

As far as Mary Jo knew, she was the first Stolle blood relative to develop cancer of the breast. Later, a relative asserted that her great-grandmother, Anna Mary Stolle, had breast cancer; it's unclear whether that is true. The words, "carcinoma of," are visible on Anna's 1934 death certificate, but the next word is illegible. Still, even if Anna did have breast cancer, that family history may not have been influential in Mary Jo's case. It's hard to pin down what factors may have culminated in breast cancer for her. That's also true for many other people with cancer: it's often hard to figure out *why* cancer strikes.

After doctors found Mary Jo's cancer, her own mortality smacked her in the face. A woman of deep Christian faith, she knew that her ultimate destiny rested in God's hands. Still, Mary Jo resolved: She would maximize whatever time she had left on this planet. She would focus on things that she could control. And she would devote her time and energy to things that mattered: mostly her family, followed closely by her dearest friends. The future seemed suffocatingly uncertain.

"In her private moments, she would break down and cry, and say, 'I'm always thinking: Will I be here in a year?' But she wouldn't do that in front of other people," her daughter, Amy, said. She never wanted others to feel uncomfortable about her illness; she didn't want people to feel sorry for her.

Deep down inside, Mary Jo worried that she might never get to see her children, Amy and Spence, get married and have their own children—her grandchildren.

"Before I even got married, she was sewing a baby blanket," Amy said. "So, there was that pressure—I need to get married and have a baby so she can hold it."

But Mary Jo would, in fact, live to see both Amy and Spence walk down the aisle—and she also would experience the joys of loving five grandchildren.

In the meantime, Mary Jo grabbed big fistfuls of life each day, embracing the axiom: "tomorrow is never promised."

Mary Jo loved teaching so much, she was determined to keep doing it even while enduring chemotherapy—a labor of love that touched her Lebanon school district colleagues, such as Pam Hatfield Russell.

Pam looked up to Mary Jo, even though Pam had been teaching for nine years by the time the two of them met in August 1991. "From the moment I first met her, I loved her," Pam said.

Pam was a fourth-grade teacher at Francis Dunlavy Elementary and Mary Jo was a part-time tutor.

Later, the women reconnected when both were teaching at Alfred Holbrook Elementary School in August 1992, several months after Mary Jo had been diagnosed with cancer. "I was her number-one fan," Pam said. She admired Mary Jo for tutoring while also assuming a regular classroom-teaching job with third graders. On top of that, Mary Jo was in the midst of cancer treatments—and conditions at Holbrook were rather inhospitable. The building, which now houses the school district's administrative offices, was constructed in 1959, the same year Mary Jo graduated from Lebanon High. And when she and Pam taught at Holbrook, the building had no air conditioning. During warm weather, the building was sweltering inside.

"It was almost unbearable for people who *weren't* sick, and here was this sweet lady, just sweating miserably as a side effect from the medicines she was taking, and then having to teach in a classroom that was so hot," Pam said. "I remember being so sad every time I saw her in that situation, I just wanted to give her a big squeeze."

Pam couldn't stand seeing Mary Jo suffer like that, so she approached Mary Jo and told her, "You are an amazing teacher. I am pretty sure that they can get an air-conditioning unit for your classroom." But Mary Jo balked. Pam remembers her response: "I don't want them making any exceptions for me."

But Pam was adamant. She told Mary Jo that asking for an air conditioner was a reasonable request. Mary Jo stood her ground, and replied: "You know, Pam, I can't do that." Pam said she could ask on Mary Jo's behalf.

"But Mary Jo was having no part of that," Pam said. "She just said, no, it wouldn't be fair for her to have air-conditioning when other teachers didn't."

The silent message: Even though some people considered Mary Jo to be "Lebanon royalty," she never expected special treatment. Not even during one of the most trying times of her life.

Mary Jo's daughter, Amy, said she knew her mother worked in less-than-ideal conditions at Holbrook. "But that class was

Mary Jo adored her students at Alfred Holbrook Elementary School in Lebanon, Ohio.

so special to her. It gave her something to focus on, and the kids were making her feel young," Amy said. "She was helping them—and they were helping her."

It was especially touching when a student named Ty declared that he was going to get his head shaved to show solidarity with Mary Jo when chemotherapy caused her hair to fall out. "He tried to instigate the other kids to shave their heads, too," Amy said. That didn't happen. But Mary Jo was touched by Ty's sweet intentions, Mary Jo's son, Spence, said: "She thought it was so neat that an eight-year-old boy would stand up and say that he and the other kids were going to do that."

In the winter months, Mary Jo felt more comfortable in class than she did in the summer—but some of her students didn't. "She would notice that some of the kids were lacking appropriate clothing—just small jackets instead of winter coats," Pam said. "You take for granted that everyone has a winter coat, but not everybody does. And Mary Jo's little heart would just melt for those kids."

Unbeknownst to those children, Mary Jo found a way to help them: She would shop for coats and would get other people to deliver them to the needy children, Pam said, adding, "I think she even helped out those kids' families. She was—wow—something special."

Pam loved Mary Jo's personality, too. She always seemed to be smiling, and Pam sensed "a kind of orneriness" in Mary Jo. "She'd get tickled and just laugh," Pam said. "I remember doing that together when we were teaching."

Pam also marveled at how Mary Jo related to her students as an educator. "Seeing how she was with the kids, I felt like she was able to pull information from them, to get them to do a lot of the things that she wanted them to do," Pam said.

Even kids who "just weren't very kind to others" seemed to behave better for Mary Jo, Pam said. "She was able to communicate with them on life skills, along with the teaching part—just how to be a good person." Something about Mary Jo's demeanor made kids eager to please her, Pam said: "She just came across to them in a way that made them feel like they didn't want to disappoint her."

Mary Jo seemed "motherly," Pam said: "She took such an interest in her students. She just loved those kids like they were her own."

Mary Jo's son and daughter both used similar words to describe their mother's regard for her students. Spence said their mom was especially excited to be working full-time again, after he and Amy were grown up. "She really embraced it like she was a first-year teacher," he said.

Because Mary Jo was so enthusiastic, patient and creative with her students, Spence said no one who knew her would ever doubt that she had chosen the right profession: "She was *made* to be a teacher—completely."

In a 1991 Lebanon school record, Mary Jo wrote that she felt fortunate to be doing what she "most wanted to do:" working with young children. And, she said, "I can't think of anything more personally rewarding."

As a teacher, Mary Jo was acutely aware of the power of knowledge. So one day, when her sister-in-law, Ginny Kuntz, accompanied Mary Jo to one of her initial cancer-treatment sessions, Mary Jo said she wanted to go to a bookstore. Ginny remembers Mary Jo telling her why: "I need to get every book I can find about breast cancer. I need to educate myself. I need to know more about myself than a doctor does." Mary Jo left the store with an armload of books. She later would use that knowledge to help her decide which treatments to undergo, and to decipher the sometimes-technical language that doctors would use. She also would share what she knew with other cancer patients, including friends and relatives who were later diagnosed.

As much as Mary Jo wanted to learn about cancer, she knew that it wasn't good to think about it all the time. So besides focusing on her students and her family, Mary Jo also took on a big personal task: moving out of the house where Amy and Spence had grown up. "You would think that would be overwhelming, but it gave her something else to occupy her mind," Amy said.

Mary Jo and Robbie left behind their longtime residence at 7401 Kings Run Road, which was built in 1964, and upgraded to a larger, newer home at 10335 Apple Park Court, a 4,300-square-foot, two-story that was built in 1990, just two years before they bought it. Both homes were in the Centerville/Washington Township, Ohio area, about six miles apart.

Not long after relocating, Mary Jo completed her course of chemotherapy. To celebrate—and to thank about a dozen of her closest friends for their support—she held a luncheon at Sycamore Creek Country Club nearby. Beforehand, Amy and her mother shared a private moment. Amy presented her mother with a gold "my angel" good-luck charm that she had purchased from Things Remembered, a shopping-mall store that specialized in personalized gifts.

Mary Jo attached that charm to her purse and carried it with her from that time forward, a sweet token of her daughter's love, concern and hope.

In spring 1993, a few months after celebrating the end of her chemo, Mary Jo made a difficult decision: To have doctors remove her right breast, even though there was no sign of cancer there. "She was just afraid of it spreading," Ginny said, adding that she knew that Mary Jo's husband, Robbie, supported her decision. Ginny recalled that Robbie had told Mary Jo: "I don't love you because of your chest. I love you because of *you*." He encouraged her to do what she thought was right for her body.

Although the situation was serious—one that can cause emotional upheaval for many women—Mary Jo injected a bit of ironic humor. A small-breasted lady, Mary Jo said that she had little to lose by having a second mastectomy—echoing a witty remark that First Lady Nancy Reagan shared in a 1988 *New York Times* article. Mrs. Reagan recounted telling doctors in October 1987 that she wanted an immediate mastectomy if they found cancer. "It won't take you long, because I was never Dolly Parton," Mrs. Reagan quipped, referring to the buxom country music star.

By opting for a mastectomy right away, Mrs. Reagan drew criticism. Some experts argued that removing just the cancerous lump might have sufficed; some worried that Mrs. Reagan was setting a wrong example for women who might not need such a drastic procedure. Decades later, she stood by her decision. Mrs. Reagan revealed that part of her rationale was that the mastectomy would enable her to avoid the rigors of radiation and/or chemotherapy, leaving her more available to assist with her husband's presidential duties. Mrs. Reagan outlived her husband. She died of heart failure in 2016 at the age of 94—with no recurrence of cancer in twenty-eight years.

The decision to have a mastectomy is a very individual one, based on many medical, emotional and personal considerations. In recent years, some women have opted for breast removal even without having cancer first. That was the case with actress Angelina Jolie. In 2013, she underwent a preventative double mastectomy at age 37. Because her mother had died from ovarian cancer at age 56, Jolie underwent genetic testing—and discovered she had a mutation that gave her an 87 percent chance of developing breast cancer. Jolie's double mastectomy wouldn't guarantee she was safe from breast cancer, but it would reduce her risk to 5 percent. That's according to an opinion piece Jolie wrote about her experience for the *New York Times* shortly after her surgeries were done. "Cancer is still a word that strikes fear into people's hearts, producing a deep sense of powerlessness," Jolie wrote. "But today it is possible to find out through a blood test whether you are highly susceptible to breast and ovarian cancer, and then take action." She encouraged women to seek information and experts to help them make "informed choices" based on their own circumstances.

After the double mastectomy, Jolie underwent reconstructive surgery with breast implants—something Mary Jo didn't do.

A few months before Mary Jo's diagnosis, the U.S. Food and Drug Administration had issued a moratorium on silicone gel-filled breast implants, citing concerns about the devices rupturing, causing pain or sparking immune-system disorders. That moratorium was lifted in 2006. Although saline-filled implants were still OK for use around the time of Mary Jo's diagnosis, Mary Jo's best friend from college, Martie Mehallis, said she thinks Mary Jo preferred to conserve her energy for fighting cancer instead of expending it to recover from cosmetic surgery. Considering all the circumstances, Martie doubts Mary Jo gave much thought to getting breast implants—a decision that, much like a mastectomy decision, is a personal and emotional one.

A few months after Mary Jo had her second mastectomy, all appeared to be well; there was no sign of a recurrence. She completed the 1992–93 school year and had intended to go back to teaching. But her two surgeries and the battery of medications had taken a toll. To recharge herself and to continue with preventative medications, Mary Jo took a leave of absence from her teaching job for the 1993–94 school year.

Still, the future was looking brighter for Mary Jo.

On November 13, 1993, the football team from her son's college, the Indiana University Hoosiers, traveled to Columbus, Ohio, to face off against Mary Jo's Ohio State Buckeyes. So Spence showed up to surprise his mom. Mary Jo and her husband, Robbie, were season-ticket holders who routinely went to the games with family and friends. On that particular night, the group ended up having dinner and singing karaoke at a Columbus nightspot. "I think we closed the place down," Spence said, a smile spreading across his face as he reminisced.

Spirits were high on that memorable night. Mary Jo felt like she was celebrating the end of her cancer journey—or so she hoped.

While Mary Jo was on leave from teaching, she stayed busy "focusing not on her, but on somebody else," her daughter, Amy, said. "She was always reaching out to somebody with cancer and trying to figure out, 'How can I make it better for them?'"

Mary Jo was heavily involved in a cancer support group that started at her church, Lebanon Presbyterian, around the time she was finishing chemotherapy. Nancy Sholder, the Kettering hospital nurse who prayed with Mary Jo right after her diagnosis, was also a lay minister at the church. After seeing six parishioners, including Mary Jo, diagnosed with various types of cancer that year, Nancy collaborated with the church's associate pastor to form the cancer support group.

Nancy remembers what it was like when Mary Jo and the rest of the group met for the first time in November 1992: "I just remember the overwhelming support and friendship that happened when we gathered those six people together at the same time, who were in treatment, preparing to go through treatment, or had just finished treatment."

The group, which was open to the community at large, would remain vital for the next eleven years, disbanding only after Nancy left her position with the church.

The longer Nancy knew Mary Jo, the more she loved and respected her. "Regardless of people's economic, education or cultural background, Mary Jo exuded kindness and love to everyone—at those support-group meetings—and *always*," Nancy said.

When Mary Jo learned that people in the group were facing financial hardships because of treatment costs and lost wages, "she would slip a couple hundred dollars in an envelope, anonymously," Nancy said. Then Mary Jo would hand the money to Nancy or to another person to deliver. The recipients would respond with disbelief, often wondering aloud, "Who would be this kind to me?" Nancy said. "Just imagine how many times she probably did that for other situations."

Nancy could see that Mary Jo genuinely cared about people. Nancy felt as though she and Mary Jo were "kindred spirits" in that regard. Both had chosen to work in helping professions—Nancy, as a nurse, and Mary Jo, as a teacher. The two women were also the same age, born only six weeks apart. And they couldn't help but become emotionally close during the group's heartfelt discussions.

One particularly gut-wrenching situation involved a group member named Becky. After ovarian cancer left her too sick to come to group meetings, Mary Jo and Nancy drove about an hour east of Lebanon to visit Becky.

"The drive was just filled with expectation of seeing Becky and excitement to be with her," Nancy said. During the visit, Becky told them she found comfort in a *Bible* verse, Psalms 91:4, "He will cover you with his feathers, and under His wings you will find refuge." That stuck with Mary Jo and Nancy. So did Becky's deteriorated condition.

As Mary Jo and Nancy drove back toward Lebanon, the mood turned somber. "We talked about how we knew we would not see Becky again—and how difficult it was," Nancy said. Her voice cracked as she continued: "Both of us were touched when we left there. We talked about how we would want other people to remember us. Above all, we said we would want our families to remember our love for them." Sadly, Becky did pass away soon after that emotional visit, Nancy said.

In 1997, the support group decided to condense its collective wisdom into a twenty-six-page booklet. The local newspaper, *The Western Star,* ran an article about the group's effort under the headline, "Cancer survivors learn to find hope, peace." A photograph shows Nancy, Mary Jo and three other women assembling the booklets. They punched holes into forest-green heavyweight paper covers and white interior pages, then threaded a light-yellow ribbon through the holes and hand-tied a knot on each one.

Entitled "A Gift of Hope: Inspirational Thoughts for Cancer Survivors," the booklet is filled with cancer patients' thoughts on topics such as:

Fear and Shock. *The "C-word," no one wants to hear it...Am I going to die? "Cancer"—what a scary word!*

Anger and Disbelief. *Why me? Am I being punished for something I have done or not done during my life?... Any minute now, they will be in to tell me the results were incorrect...I'm going to awaken from this nightmare and none of this will have happened.*

Attitude. *A life-threatening illness can give wisdom that has no other source; you make sure those you love know how you feel about them.*

Acceptance and Peace. *God brought my life to a standstill so I might learn that what is really important is what I do for others. Know this: You can never be frightened again; you have experienced the worst kind of fear.*

Shortly after the booklet was published, Mary Jo distanced herself from the group somewhat. "She just needed to step back from being consumed with cancer and other people's lives; she needed a respite," Nancy said. "We all do."

But the very last message in that booklet would continue to guide Mary Jo for the rest of her days: *Today well-lived makes tomorrow a vision of hope.*

Milestones and Memories

"Making memories" became Mary Jo Cropper's post-diagnosis mantra. Hyper-focused on the important people in her life, Mary Jo took lots of pictures and lovingly wrote personal notes. She planned more vacations. And she milked every last ounce of joy out of each day. All the while, Mary Jo did her best to keep thoughts of cancer locked away in a corner of her mind, where they wouldn't taint the happy milestones that were lining up in her life.

One of the most remarkable events happened on May 15, 1994. On that date, Mary Jo and her husband, Robbie, witnessed the wedding of their two dear friends who had high school crushes on each other, Dick Zecher and the former Joan MacCallum. Their love had been on hold for thirty-five years.

The marriage of Dick and Joan might never have happened if not for a little nudge from Mary Jo. After high school, Dick and Joan had gone their separate ways; both had moved outside Ohio. In 1991, Joan came back home to Lebanon, Ohio, for a visit. That's when Mary Jo told Joan that she thought Dick, who was then married, was on the verge of becoming a free man again. Mary Jo showed Joan a video of Dick. And Joan's heart melted. "He looked adorable in that video," Joan said. A sense of "unfinished business" overtook her, she said. Soon, she and Dick "found each other again."

Three years later, Mary Jo and Robbie were among eighty guests who were invited to a three-day wedding celebration with Dick and Joan. The group gathered in the city where Dick and Joan had reconnected, New York. Friday night: a welcome dinner. Saturday night: a dinner cruise on the Hudson River and

Mary Jo and Robbie Cropper, their niece, Sylvia Norris, center, and the Croppers' children, Amy and Spence, went on the first of many ocean cruises in 1992. Mary Jo's post-cancer mantra became: "making memories."

New York Harbor. Sunday: the marriage ceremony at a prestigious venue, The Plaza Hotel. Mary Jo, whose cancer was in remission, beamed with pride knowing she had a hand in bringing the two lovebirds together.

The new Mr. and Mrs. Zecher felt grateful and blessed to have Mary Jo, Robbie and so many dear friends there. In 2019, the Zechers, who made their home in Arizona, celebrated their twenty-fifth wedding anniversary. Joan said their relationship is still "beyond wonderful." She and Dick remain grateful for Mary Jo's benevolent intervention. "We just feel so incredibly blessed to have this 'second chance,'" Joan said.

Love also was in the air for Mary Jo's father, Ralph Stolle. He had already outlived two wives when he met a Warren County court judge, Kathleen Porter, who also had been widowed. In 1993, Ralph and Kathleen got married. The family readily accepted Kathleen; she described Mary Jo as "a lovely woman." Kathleen accompanied Ralph on business trips to foreign countries. But she, like his previous two wives and much of his family, was kept in the dark about Ralph's business and financial dealings, including the cancer research he had funded.

And Ralph didn't let people see he was upset by Mary Jo's cancer diagnosis. To him, Mary Jo's illness was a problem that needed a solution. So, relatives say, Ralph had some of Mary Jo's DNA and/or malignant tissue preserved for research purposes. But, as of early 2020, none of Ralph's surviving relatives or business associates knew what, if anything, resulted from those efforts.

Likewise, no one seems to know details of how Ralph treated his own cancer after he was diagnosed in 1994. When Mary Jo resigned from the Lebanon schools in June 1995, following two consecutive school years of medical leave, she attributed her resignation partly to her father's illness. Six months later, Ralph died of cancer. Ralph had been so fascinated with cancer research that he clipped and saved many newspaper articles on that topic. Stacks of those articles, yellowed with age, are included among the personal documents his family kept after his death.

His widow, Kathleen, recalls how Mary Jo and the entire family reacted when Ralph passed away on January 13, 1996: "There was a deep, deep sorrow, but then joy and relief that he was going home to be with the Lord," Kathleen said.

As sad as his relatives were, they recognized that Ralph had lived an extraordinarily long and fulfilling life. He had lived to age 91; his funeral was held on January 17, 1996, which would have been his 92nd birthday. In an article published on that date, the man who was then Ohio's governor, George Voinovich, called Ralph Stolle "one of the finest gentlemen I had ever met." Voinovich also lauded Ralph as an "unsung entrepreneur in Ohio's history." Mostly without fanfare, Ralph had accomplished more in one lifetime than some families do in several generations. In that same article, *The Western Star* newspaper noted that, a few weeks before he died, Ralph had received an award that touched his heart and brought tears to his eyes: The Presbyterian Altar Guild's GLOW Award, presented to a person whose "light shines as bright as an example of what God intended us to be," the article described, adding, "the world is brighter because of your inner glow." Once again, this was a description that would also have been befitting of his daughter, Mary Jo.

Shortly after his death, the family had to push past grief of losing Ralph so they could prepare for a joyous occasion: the marriage of Mary Jo's daughter, Amy—to Dale Settlemyre, a man she met through her mother's apparently habitual matchmaking.

Dale's mother, Patricia, had been diagnosed with cancer. After Pat joined the Lebanon Presbyterian Church cancer support group in 1994, Mary Jo volunteered to drive Pat to Columbus, Ohio, for treatments. During the car trips, the two women had long conversations; they discovered they had a lot in common. Both had graduated from Ohio State. Both loved playing card games. And they both had deep roots in the Warren County farming community. In fact, Pat's family owned a farming business close to SanMarGale, Settlemyre Seed Company, and Ralph Stolle knew the family. Yet the two women's paths hadn't crossed prior to the support-group meeting. After the two moms got together, "they got to talking about their two kids who weren't dating anyone at the time," Amy said, referring to herself and to Pat's son, Dale. "Six months later, he ended up calling me."

The couple started dating in April 1995; before long, a wedding date was on the calendar: March 16, 1996.

Mary Jo relished the preparations. "She never had that big wedding, so she was happy to do that for me," Amy said. "She joked that she was 'the wedding planner' and she instructed each of the groomsmen on what they needed to do that day."

Amy stepped back and let her mother enjoy all the hustle-and-bustle. Because of her mother's cancer diagnosis, Amy could see that it had become extra-important for her mom to add special touches to every aspect of life that she could. As her mother had requested, Amy had wedding photos shot at The Gables, the historic Cropper home.

Grandpa Stolle's recent passing left a void, but Amy incorporated his presence into the wedding. She purchased her wedding gown with money he had given to her—and paid homage to him with a soloist singing, "I Believe," an uplifting 1953 tune that Ralph loved.

And the wedding was held at the church that was so important to Grandpa Stolle and to Amy's mother: Lebanon Presbyterian. So many important moments in the family's history centered around the church. It was where Ralph Stolle's visitation drew more than 500 mourners; it is where a bronze plaque honors the Stolle family for funding the bell tower's restoration in 1985, in memory of Dorothy Stolle; it was where both of Mary Jo's children, Amy and Spence, had been baptized. Now, it was where Amy was getting married. And soon, that church would be where Spence would have his wedding, too.

For almost as long as she can remember, Dana VanDeGrift had known the Cropper family. She grew up in Lebanon, where her dad, Jim, was a successful and respected coach of the high school football team. Because of connections between that team and the Cropper family, the VanDeGrifts were invited to go to Lake Cumberland with Ginny Kuntz, Spence Cropper's aunt. That happened sometime after 1979. That's the year when actress Bo Derek appeared in the movie *10* with her hair meticulously plaited into dozens of braids, a bead dangling from the end of each one. And Dana remembers she was sporting the Bo Derek hairstyle, courtesy of her sister's braiding skills, when she went to Lake Cumberland and met Spence Cropper for the first time. The meeting was unremarkable otherwise. She and Spence were just little kids, and Spence was attending school in Centerville, thirteen miles from Dana's school district, Lebanon.

Although Spence and Dana got along well, and they were both born in 1972, "the timing was never right for us to get together," Dana said. "We were both always seeing other people." And, for a time, Dana lived in Florida, hundreds of miles away.

But in 1997, a traumatic event pulled Dana back home. Her dad was nearly killed when his tractor exploded, causing a fire that burned 80 percent of his body. He remained hospitalized from June until September that year. The Lebanon community responded with help from every direction and renamed the school's football stadium in his honor. *Faith Through Flames: The Jim VanDeGrift Story* by Joe Henderson (Amazon.com, 2019), tells the miraculous, inspirational tale.

Shortly after her dad's accident, Dana returned to live in Lebanon; like Mary Jo, Dana was a schoolteacher. That commonality alone endeared Dana to Mary Jo. But Mary Jo also loved Dana's upbeat, pleasant personality and her solid religious foundation. Likewise, Dana's mom, Rosie VanDeGrift, liked everything that she knew about Spence and his family.

The two moms hatched a plan to bring their children together. "Rosie and Mary Jo set us up; we were like an arranged marriage," Dana said in hindsight, laughing. "It's funny how they 'played' us."

One day, Dana's mother, Rosie, nonchalantly asked her: "What do you think of Spencer Cropper? He seems like he's a lot of fun." Dana responded affirmatively but seemed a little noncommittal. Then Rosie told Mary Jo about the conversation, leading Mary Jo to declare to Spence: "You need to call Dana VanDeGrift. She's expecting you to call her." Like a good son, Spence complied.

Soon, Spence and Dana were on their first date: a December 1997 dinner at The Precinct, a premier fine-dining restaurant in Cincinnati, followed by attending a performance of *The Nutcracker* ballet, a Christmas classic.

The next thing Spence and Dana knew, they were getting married.

"Those kids didn't have a chance. Their mothers were too powerful," Ginny said.

Dana was happy to be getting Mary Jo as her mother-in-law because she was so fond of her.

"I remember thinking, 'I want to be like her.' She was classy and kind; she wasn't flashy. She was elegant and sophisticated without being arrogant," Dana said. "She was warm, and she didn't forget what was important to you."

And Dana thought it was cute that, while she and Spence were planning their wedding, Mary Jo joked that "the mother of the groom is supposed to wear beige and keep her mouth shut." Mary Jo only made one request, Dana recalls: The obligatory wedding portraits at The Gables.

Although Mary Jo did end up wearing a beige dress, in a photo taken at the wedding on July 3, 1999, the color didn't make

Mary Jo and Robbie Cropper were thrilled when their son, Spence, married the former Dana VanDeGrift—a result of Mary Jo's matchmaking.

her disappear into the woodwork. In her own low-key way, Mary Jo still stood out—even while wearing beige. Fancy lace accented the top of Mary Jo's full-length gown; in a picture taken at the church, she has a healthy glow and a broad smile as she poses next to her son, the groom. He was all grown up, standing six feet, five inches—ten inches taller than his mother. Still, Mary Jo's positive energy magnetized people to her, even without her trying. "Mary Jo just had this warm sparkle," Dana said. "If you saw her in a group of people, if you didn't know who she was, you would notice her and *want* to know who she was."

Spence and Dana's wedding day was a particularly emotional one for Mary Jo, partly because she very much disliked being the center of attention, even for a few moments. "At our wedding, she was just so daggone nervous because she had to walk down the aisle in front of people," Dana said. Mary Jo also was having a tough time marrying off her last child, whose personality closely mirrored hers. Years later, in an email to a friend, Mary Jo described how she felt about her children's weddings: Being the mother of the bride involved more responsibilities; being the mother of the groom seemed more intense. "I guess it was hard giving 'my little boy' up," Mary Jo wrote.

Shortly after Spence and Dana were married, Mary Jo touched Dana's heart by presenting her with a "back-to-school" giftbag. It contained an apple, a wristwatch and a teacher's sweater from BellePointe, a novelty clothier with a Columbus location that specialized in Ohio State apparel. Twenty years later, Dana still has the handwritten note that Mary Jo enclosed in the giftbag. Dana treasures the note as a reminder of her mother-in-law's thoughtful, playful nature. "Happy new school year, Mrs. Cropper," Mary Jo wrote, honoring Dana's newlywed status. Then Mary Jo added a humorous explanation for one of the gifts, saying, "The watch will help you keep track of important times during the school day: lunch, planning period and dismissal."

Mary Jo signed the note with a stylized signature she had adopted over the years: a smiley face with a "halo" swirled above it, representing an angel—a symbol that would grow increasingly important to Mary Jo, to her family and to total strangers who followed in her footsteps.

After her children got married, Mary Jo hoped that grandchildren would be making appearances soon. She got her wish.

The day before Amy and Dale celebrated their first wedding anniversary, Amy gave birth to Mary Jo's first grandchild, Alison Settlemyre, in 1997. Coincidentally, Amy also had been born within a day of her parents' wedding anniversary, except her birth came a year and one day *after* Robbie and Mary Jo had remarried.

Mary Jo was so excited about Amy's baby coming, she stayed with her daughter during twenty hours of labor at Bethesda

North Hospital near Cincinnati. After the baby, nicknamed Ali, was born, when Amy's husband went to tell the rest of the family, "it's a girl," Mary Jo made a beeline to see Amy with the newborn. "My mom literally raced into the room. She was going to be the first one in there—before my mother-in-law or anyone else—and you couldn't hold her back," Amy said, laughing at the memory. "It was a very special day in her life."

Mary Jo cried tears of joy. Considering that she was then five years into her cancer's remission, Mary Jo felt particularly blessed; she had lived to see little Ali swaddled in the pink-and-blue baby blanket that she had sewn years earlier to welcome that first grandchild.

Mary Jo was thrilled with her new status as "grandma," but wasn't wild about being labeled that way. She wanted to be called by a "special name," Amy said. So, soon after Ali could talk, she came up with a nickname for Mary Jo: "Mimi." And rather than calling Mary Jo's husband, Robbie, "grandpa," Ali dubbed him, "Pa."

Those nicknames stuck; they were used by the four other grandchildren who followed. Amy and Dale's son, Drew, was born in May 2000. He got loads of attention because the rest of Mary Jo's grandchildren were girls; he ended up being the only boy.

That December, Spence and Dana welcomed the firstborn of their three daughters, Josephine, also known as Josie, at Bethesda North.

Mary Jo seemed just as excited about Josie's birth as she had been about the births of Amy's two children, Spence said: "She was just elated about having another grandchild."

And, the day after Josie's birth, when the baby needed to be taken to a nearby hospital for tests, Mary Jo drove from her Centerville home through a snowstorm to be with Dana at Bethesda. Mary Jo wanted to comfort the young, worried mother as she recovered from twenty-three hours of labor, Spence said. Although that day's snowfall accumulated a fraction of an inch, driving conditions were less-than-ideal. But Mary Jo wouldn't be deterred because she had such regard for Dana. Everyone breathed sighs of relief after all of Josie's testing turned out OK.

Mary Jo with her first grandchild, Ali Settlemyre. Ali was the first to refer to Mary Jo as "Mimi," a nickname that the other four grandchildren also used for her.

Over the next few years, when Spence's other two daughters were born, Mary Jo seemed equally enthusiastic, Spence said—even in the face of circumstances that threatened to diminish her joy.

Mary Jo's "making memories" mission included planning ocean cruises and other excursions for her friends and family. The first of those major trips happened in the summer of 1992, while Mary Jo was still undergoing her first rounds of cancer treatments. About twenty people went on that Caribbean cruise, Amy recalls. "She felt good and just wanted to be around everyone," Amy said. "And I'm sure she was thinking, 'I don't know how long I have.'" The family traveled aboard Royal Caribbean's *Monarch of the Seas* during the ship's inaugural season. Later cruises would include more than fifty people in Mary Jo's group.

Within a few years, Mary Jo began to rely on a young lady, the former Marsha Godsey, to put together those trips. Marsha already had connections with the Stolle family. After graduating from Sidney High School, Marsha went to work with computers at Stolle Precision Tools in her hometown, Sidney, Ohio, in 1988. "If you lived in Sidney, *everything* in town was 'Stolle,'" Marsha said. While Ralph's family pronounced the name, "STAL-lee," some people around Sidney said, "STOL-lee." Either way, that name was revered in Sidney, a city of about twenty thousand people, located between Dayton and Toledo. Much of that city's economy was dependent upon the Stolle businesses. Back then, there were ten Stolle plants around town, Marsha said, "and just about everyone I knew worked there."

At work, Marsha met one of Ralph Stolle's most trusted executives, Bill Falknor. He had worked for Ralph ever since he got out of the U.S. Navy in 1965. Just as a May-December romance had blossomed for Ralph and his new wife, Kathleen, a similar relationship developed between Bill and Marsha. Believing it was unwise to have a personal relationship at work, Marsha got a different job in 1993. But "the whole Stolle family accepted us from the very beginning," Bill said. By 1995, he and Marsha were married.

Then the new Mrs. Falknor joined Jones Travel, a Lebanon agency that had long been entrusted with the Stolles' corporate travel plans. Increasingly, the whole Stolle-Cropper clan, including Mary Jo, started enlisting Marsha's help for personal travel arrangements. "And it was so fun," Marsha said. "They were so easy to work with. They'd give me an idea of what they wanted, I'd research it, tell them about it and they'd say, 'That sounds wonderful—book it!'"

Mary Jo's sister-in-law, Ginny Kuntz, would also help Mary Jo coordinate travel plans; Ginny and Mary Jo seemed to go everywhere together, Marsha said.

And the two sisters-in-law established a new family tradition: Every year at Christmas, they would surprise their relatives with a big trip—and they would urge the recipients to guess that year's destination based on a gift that provided a clue, such as a pineapple ornament to represent a Hawaiian vacation or a Mickey Mouse toy to telegraph a Disney-themed trip.

"Mary Jo just loved traveling and taking all of them with her," Marsha said. "She got so much joy out of just being with her family, wherever they went."

Over the years, Mary Jo kept Marsha hopping. Because Marsha retired from her travel job and no longer has access to certain records, she can only estimate how many trips Mary Jo booked with her. But the list includes about eight cruises, five Hawaii trips, three visits to the Atlantis resort in the Bahama islands, and two vacations on the tropical islands of Turks and Caicos, in addition to about a half-dozen visits to Walt Disney World in Orlando, Florida.

But Marsha was more than just Mary Jo's travel agent. She became her friend—one whose love and admiration for Mary Jo would only intensify in the coming years, especially after an unfortunate turn of events.

Mary Jo kept a travel journal during one of her favorite trips, a 1993 visit to Hawaii with her immediate family, plus her sister-in-law, Ginny Kuntz, and her husband, Ron. The trip started in Kona, then went to several other spots, and was packed with activities ranging from a dolphin swim to a luau. There also was a dinner cruise. Mary Jo's description: "Had a ball! Amy got picked to do the hula and Dad was a riot. He was dressed as a hula girl—skirt, coconuts and all … a great time dancing."

Another highlight: the group awakened at 3 a.m. to head for Mount Haleakala. Mary Jo recorded its height—10,023 feet—and its description: "dormant volcano, largest in the world." She noted: "Arrive to see a spectacular sunrise. A real wonder—vast crater—you felt as if you were on the moon."

Because of the elevation, the temperature at dawn was about 30 degrees, she wrote. So, everyone had to get suited up to ride bicycles down the mountainside. Mary Jo said she gave up on that quest and boarded a van while the rest of her group was left to "fight the elements, wind and rain, to make it all the way." At the end of the excursion, everyone seemed a little tired "but overall enjoyed the ride and were proud they'd done it." Mary Jo said she was disappointed in herself for quitting—a rarity for her.

The next day, Mary Jo tried snorkeling for the first time—and fared better with that. "It was breathtaking," she wrote.

Mary Jo returned to Hawaii several other times, and once, on the island of Maui, she and Robbie tried the infamous Road to Hana. It's a day-long, white-knuckle drive along a narrow road with hairpin turns, carved into a cliffside. While there are spectacular views along the route to the little town called Hana, the trip can be so nerve-racking, Mary Jo joked, "The Road to Hana should be called The Road to Divorce!" She and Robbie made a joint decision: It wasn't worth the stress, so they turned back, Ginny said.

Laughter seemed to follow Mary Jo, center, with several ladies who were dear to her heart. From left: her sister, Gail Norris; sister-in-law, Ginny Kuntz; college roommate, Martie Mehallis; and pastor, Alice Petersen.

Another of Mary Jo's Hawaii trips spawned "The Wahines." That's Hawaiian for "women." And it became the nickname for a group of free-spirited ladies who went with Mary Jo on a memorable vacation.

Among those gals was Alice Petersen. While living in the Cincinnati area, she had become friends with Ginny through a Presbyterian women's retreat. Alice had moved to Pittsburgh, Pennsylvania, in 1993. But more than a half-dozen years later, Ginny invited Alice to join her, Mary Jo and others for a trip to Maui. Alice was unsure. She was only briefly acquainted with most of the other women, including Mary Jo. Still, at Ginny's urging, Alice decided to go. She traveled from Pittsburgh to meet the other ladies in Lebanon, and they drove together to the Cincinnati airport. At first, everyone felt a bit awkward because, "All of these women knew one another—and I also was a pastor," Alice said. Her title made the other gals start to worry that they might need to be on their best behavior. But Alice made it clear that her presence shouldn't inhibit them. "I wasn't wearing my 'pastor hat' with them," she said. "And we all decided that, 'what happened in Hawaii stayed in Hawaii.'"

To this day, some secrets from that decades-old trip haven't been divulged. But some photographic "evidence" does exist. A picture from that trip shows eight women posed on the deck of a boat, tanned and smiling, with the dark blue Pacific Ocean as a backdrop. Besides Alice, Ginny and Mary Jo, the group also included Mary Jo's sister, Gail Norris; her daughter-in-law's mother, Rosie VanDeGrift; Gail's schoolmate, Talitha Colston; Mary Jo's schoolmate, Marilyn Keever Long; and Jane Cantoni, a longtime friend of the family.

By the end of the vacation, Alice had been welcomed into the fold. "I came as Ginny's friend, and then became friends with each one of them as well," she said.

Alice didn't know Mary Jo very well before that trip. "Mary Jo is one of the few women that I would say this about: Mary Jo, in her simplicity, was quite elegant," Alice said. Yet that elegance wasn't cold and detached. It was warm and engaging. "I think it's well-known that Mary Jo has long, long roots in Lebanon, and came from affluence. But she didn't wear that on her sleeve at all," Alice said. "She just had an inner beauty. I always respected that about her."

Also, Alice said she made a personal "rule" that she wouldn't think of Mary Jo any differently because of her higher economic status. After all, Alice said, Mary Jo didn't allow that factor to drive a wedge between her and anyone else.

"She would have been as comfortable with someone who was homeless as she would be with someone who had great resources," Alice said. "She was always very gracious with what she had."

Without a doubt, the most special moment of the first Wahines trip was at the very end, when Alice and Ginny came up with the idea of sharing communion together just before they departed for the ten-hour flight home. Without telling the other ladies what they had planned, Alice and Ginny drove with their friends to a secluded lookout point just northeast of Kapalua, which means "arms embracing the sea."

The women walked up a slight rock incline. "The ocean was far below, and beautiful," Ginny said. They took a seat on a ledge, among soaring Cook and Norfolk Island pine trees, which were swaying in the breeze.

Then Alice and Ginny told the other women they were going to take communion right there amid the natural beauty of the Pacific coastline. "You'll find no greater cathedral than this," Alice told the women. "She's right," they murmured, beholding the sky above and the ocean below, both so vast and both so blue. It was a profound moment. Some of the women were moved to tears… until their reverie was disrupted by the sounds of sputtering and choking coming from Talitha Colston. Thinking that she was drinking *grape juice,* which Presbyterians' customarily use for communion instead of wine, Talitha had taken a huge gulp of *wine.* Although Talitha enjoys wine, the unexpected mouthful of it caused her throat to seize up. She blurted out: "I haven't had wine for communion since I was a Catholic!" Her companions cracked up.

After the hilarity subsided, the mood turned spiritual again. As the ladies walked back toward their rental cars, a scruffy-looking middle-aged Hawaiian man walked toward them and asked what the ladies were doing. They told him they were from Ohio, and they were marking their last day in Hawaii with a communion service. Then, with his arms outstretched in the air, the man proclaimed that he felt "mana," a sacred Hawaiian term meaning spiritual energy. The women were amazed that, somehow, this stranger seemed to have detected the intensity of the experience they had just shared. As the ladies left the area, they took one last look at the ocean. A whale was slapping its tail on the water. "We all remarked that he was 'waving goodbye,' or 'aloha!'" Ginny said.

It was a fitting conclusion to the first of many Wahines gatherings that blended seriousness, silliness and sisterhood.

As a result of the Wahines outings, Alice became closer with Mary Jo, but the bond they shared wasn't "really, really close," as the one between Mary Jo and Ginny was, Alice said.

However, Alice and Mary Jo had something powerful in common with Mary Jo that Ginny did not: Alice had been diagnosed with breast cancer in 1998, six years after Mary Jo's diagnosis.

Anyone who has walked along the path of a life-threatening illness gains an understanding that is hard to convey to those who, by the grace of God, haven't had such an experience.

Alice particularly recalls one phone conversation in which Mary Jo provided some valuable perspective. When Alice expressed anxiety about some test results, Mary Jo made a statement that always stayed with Alice. "In her journey with breast cancer, she told me that she had learned: 'I wouldn't worry about it, until you know what you're worrying about,'" Alice said. "That was how she had learned to live, year after year."

After their inaugural Maui outing, the Wahines shared quite a few adventures together—always with a lot of laughter and a fair amount of wine. Mary Jo was a wine enthusiast and loved sharing that passion with her friends. As of 2020, Wahines who still lived in Ohio were still getting together for lunch or dinner, Ginny said—and for sharing stories about fun times they had with Mary Jo.

When Ralph Stolle died, he left a multimillion-dollar estate that would enable Mary Jo and his other heirs to continue the philanthropic traditions he had started. But the value of Ralph's estate had been shrouded in mystery because he kept his financial status under wraps. Perhaps that was partly because Ralph was afraid that disclosing his wealth would make him more of a target; his home had been burglarized in the 1970s, prompting him to get security systems for himself and his daughters. And he probably thought that discussing money would be boastful—and that would seem gauche to him. Ralph refused to buy luxury cars because "he never wanted to drive anything that his workers couldn't afford," his daughter, Sandy Perry, said.

Whatever his rationale, Ralph was so tight-lipped about financial matters that Sandy had no idea of her father's net worth until she was 23 years old. Then a college student, Sandy met a young man who had learned, through business connections at Alcoa aluminum, that her dad was a multimillionaire. When he informed Sandy of the amount, she was in disbelief—an amount that, out of respect for Ralph's sensibilities, shall remain undisclosed.

But a few indicators of Ralph's wealth are contained in a boxful of family mementos. A typewritten chronology says Alcoa purchased The Stolle Corporation in 1977, and afterward, the Stolle subsidiary was making annual sales of $500 million, with 2,600 employees. That means the Alcoa deal alone was undoubtedly valued in the millions.

At the time of his passing, Ralph still owned a number of businesses; all three of his daughters then were appointed to the board of his main company. Because Ralph had been so secretive about his business dealings, his daughters knew nothing about the inner workings of his companies. Nevertheless, Mary Jo would show up at board meetings looking every bit the business-woman, said longtime Stolle associate Bill Falknor. "She always looked like a million dollars and was always prepared," he said. "She would come in with her tablet and take notes."

Ralph's last will and testament had given his daughters and grandsons the power to make key decisions about his assets; the family sold many of Ralph's businesses.

Ralph's estate was so complex, it took five years and more than two hundred pages of documents to finalize.

In the coming years, developers and the Stolle family put together an ambitious plan to transform Ralph's 3,335 acres into a community that would have been named SanMarGale. The proposal called for thousands of new homes, plus a village town center, public services buildings, retail shops and recreation areas. Although Warren County officials did approve the plan after a series of controversial public hearings, the development was shelved because of a downturn in the housing market. Eventually, the land returned to its original zoning designation and Ralph's heirs started selling individual parcels.

In any case, the sale of Ralph's property, companies and other assets would allow Ralph's descendants to lead comfortable lifestyles for years to come.

"To be honest, none of us had very much money until Dad passed away," said his daughter, Sandy.

With more funds to manage and a desire to use that money for good, Mary Jo decided to seek guidance from a "chartered advisor in philanthropy," or CAP. This type of financial professional helps wealthy people figure out how to best benefit themselves, their families and society. A CAP named Sally Alspaugh, now known as Sally Finn, was already working with Mary Jo's in-laws, Ginny and Ron Kuntz; the Kuntzes referred the Croppers to Sally after Ralph's death.

As a CAP, Sally had a responsibility to know more than just the numbers on her clients' balance sheets. She delved deeply into their family and individual histories, their passions, their likes and dislikes.

During 2000, shortly after first meeting Mary Jo and Robbie Cropper, Sally went to lunch with them and asked the couple a probing question: "If both of you gave away a million dollars this afternoon, would it change your lifestyle?" Both responded "no."

Sally tucked away that answer for the time being. Six years later, its true significance would become apparent.

As the calendar year flipped to 2001, Mary Jo's sixtieth birthday was on the horizon—a day she worried she might never see after being diagnosed with cancer nine years earlier.

To celebrate that milestone birthday, she decided to splurge on a limousine ride. She invited her family and a couple friends to go along. The main purpose was nostalgic: to drive past her childhood home at 21 Carolina Avenue in Fort Thomas, Kentucky.

But a couple funny things happened during the limo ride. While driving in Mary Jo's old neighborhood, the limo driver turned into a driveway—and got stuck. "It was such a tight fit that it took quite some time and effort to turn us around," Spence said.

Then there was Mary Jo's spur-of-the-moment decision that inspired peals of laughter years later.

Although most people who knew Mary Jo would describe her as "a classy lady," she would sometimes crave a low-budget fast-food sandwich: "sliders," steamed miniature burgers from White

Castle. She especially liked them after Ohio State football games. Truth be told, her husband, Robbie, would sometimes complain about the pungency of those little onion-y burgers lingering in the family vehicle. Nevertheless, right there in the limo, during her birthday celebration, Mary Jo got a hankering for sliders. And, as requested, the driver pulled the limousine into the White Castle drive-through in Covington, Kentucky—a jaw-dropping sight for passersby.

"It was fun," Amy said, "and it was just like her to do something like that."

And, in terms of making memories, that limo ride became one of Mary Jo's biggest successes; it was extraordinarily memorable. But just around the corner, Mary Jo was about to encounter the roughest part of her journey.

6

Illuminating the Darkness

After celebrating her sixtieth birthday cancer-free, Mary Jo believed the disease was mostly in her rearview mirror. She was still taking preventive medications and also was working on cancer-outreach activities; in 2000, she had co-chaired Warren County's first-ever "Relay for Life," an event that raised $102,000 for the American Cancer Society.

But she believed she may have wriggled out of cancer's clutches. As of spring 2001, nine years had passed without a recurrence of her cancer. And, as conventional wisdom held, if Mary Jo could hit the magic ten-year cancer-free benchmark in 2002, she had a good chance of never seeing the disease rear its ugly head again.

Instead, just as the typical car-mirror warning says, cancer was closer than it appeared to be.

In hindsight, her son, Spence, remembered how odd it seemed when his mother described a strange sensation in her body during the latter part of 2001. He and his wife, Dana, were riding with Mary Jo in her white Lexus when she reported: "I just ache. I'm just sore. My bones just hurt." But everyone dismissed the symptoms as being just normal aches and pains that come with age, with illness or sometimes, from just moving the wrong way. Or maybe it was a side effect of one of her medicines, they reasoned.

But in January 2002, when Mary Jo went for a screening, doctors shared the awful news: cancer was back—with a vengeance.

Mary Jo's pernicious adversary had wormed its way through her body, just when she and her family thought she was tantalizingly close to being "in the clear," as much as a cancer patient can be.

"If you remain in complete remission for five years or more, some doctors may say that you are cured," the National Cancer Institute says. Still, cancer cells can remain in a person's body for many years, and they might take hold again. But that usually happens within the first five years after treatment. Regardless, doctors cannot guarantee that a patient is "cured" after a certain number of cancer-free years, the institute says. "The most they can say is that there are no signs of cancer at this time."

Holding hands with a fellow participant in the "Relay for Life" cancer fundraiser that she organized, Mary Jo waves for the camera.

Here was Mary Jo, approaching her ten-year anniversary, with cancer labeled "incurable but treatable." The ticking timebomb inside of her had activated. Doctors wouldn't tell Mary Jo whether she had days, weeks, months, or years to live. But she knew, from that point forward, "she would never be without cancer again," Spence said.

Mary Jo was tempted to omit this terrible turn of events from the journal that she was writing for her soon-to-arrive granddaughter. Dana and Spence were expecting Sophia, already nicknamed "Sophie," to be born in the spring of 2002, around the time of Mary Jo's ten-year cancer anniversary.

Mary Jo had made a practice of writing journals and personal notes for all of her grandchildren. She wanted her beloved "grands" to be able to look back on her expressions of love for them, even after she was gone. After becoming Mimi to three grandchildren, with a fourth one on the way, Mary Jo had started to feel hopeful that she might live to see those grandchildren grow up and become parents of her great-grandchildren.

The re-diagnosis disintegrated that hope. Mary Jo decided to record her thoughts in a spiral-bound book with a butterfly-and-flowers design on the outside cover.

On the inside cover, Mary Jo inscribed a dedication.

To Sophie from Grandma Mimi: How I love writing these little journals. (I'm certainly getting <u>lots</u> of practice.) I hope someday you will enjoy reading it and share it with your children—know you were loved by all of us the minute we knew about you. Grow up to share that love with all those around you. God bless, Mimi

Amid descriptions of ordinary days, the entry dated January 3, 2002, stands out.

Dear little Sophie: It's been a terribly strange and difficult day for me. I thought about not sharing it, but my little journal is meant for you to get to know all of us—the ups and the downs, that make us what we are.

Almost 10 years ago, I was diagnosed with breast cancer. I was so terribly frightened of my future, but I made it. I had surgery, some by choice, took treatments and have been healthy, as I said, for almost 10 years. Now my breast cancer has reoccurred in the bone and possibly other areas. Once again, I'm devastated and so fearful of my future. I have all of you and your mommie, daddy, aunt Amy, uncle Dale, Ali and Drew and Pa, that I don't want to leave. I want to see you born, grow up, graduate, marry.

Your daddy came up and held me and he prayed. I know with the love of family and comfort of friends, I will become strong and face what must be done. I must pray to feel God's arms around me, giving me the strength I need to accept what is His will.

I will pray, too, that you are strong, and that soon I will be smiling into your smiley face. I love you—always remember that. My family is what I lived for...they are my legacy.

Goodnight, Sweetie.

The words seemed to flow directly from Mary Jo's heart to her pen. In language simple enough for a child to understand,

Mary Jo had powerfully summed up so much: her fears and her dreams, her illness and her health, her love for her family and her faith in God.

Years later, that journal has fulfilled its purpose: ensuring memories of Mimi and her undying affection stayed close to Sophie. Seventeen years later, that journal was displayed on a shelf in Sophie's bedroom. Sophie retrieved the journal and smoothed her long, blond hair behind an ear. Then, she turned to the pivotal entry about the cancer diagnosis and flawlessly read her Mimi's words aloud to a total stranger.

Asked how she felt about the journal, Sophie declared: "I just feel loved and so special to have a grandma who loved me that much and shared all of that."

Tears flowed from the eyes of everyone who witnessed that moment with Sophie in late 2019.

Sophie's mom, Dana, said Mary Jo would have been so proud of Sophie's poised recitation, considering that Mimi had helped Sophie hone her reading skills with flashcards when she was a little girl. Dana smiled at the memory of Mimi helping Sophie that way, treating her to a Happy Meal from McDonald's restaurant each time. Sophie had some learning difficulties for a while, possibly lingering effects from her birth. The umbilical cord had been wrapped around her neck, depriving her of oxygen. But under Mary Jo's tutelage, Sophie's skills soared; she ascended to a reading level that was considered "advanced," Dana said.

The final entry Mary Jo wrote in the journal for Sophie was dated Easter 2003. That was just before Sophie turned 1 year old. Mimi left these thoughts:

> *Mommie and Daddy love you dearly. Appreciate them as the loving, guiding, disciplining parents they are. They will always be there for you, Sophie, to grow in faith, love, joy, trust. We, too, will be here, or just a little prayer away.*
> *God bless you and keep you, Sophie.*
> *Much, much love,*
> *Mimi*

Despite the clarity of her words in Sophie's journal, Mary Jo felt like nothing was clear to her anymore. She was in disbelief about the cancer recurring. She was confused and frightened. She knew she needed to hear the facts about her condition, but she didn't feel like her mind would absorb them. So, Mary Jo did something she had rarely done in the past: She enlisted her husband and children to come along to a doctor's appointment. Together, they would figure out what she was facing—and what could possibly be done about it.

"I remember her calling and saying, 'It's back … and I want you to go to the doctor with me. I want you to be my eyes and ears,'" Spence said.

He, his dad, Robbie, and his sister, Amy, all went to a cancer specialist's office in suburban Cincinnati in early 2002. At that point, the family knew little other than "things have changed," Amy said. All four of them braced for the news, knowing it would be bad—and dreading to hear how bad it really was.

"The cancer was pretty much head-to-toe," Spence said. "It wasn't in any of her organs, except for a little spot in her liver. But it was in her bones, all over the place."

That description made the entire family cringe. They were distraught. And afraid for Mary Jo.

Amy remembers the doctor classifying her mother's cancer as Stage IV. With cancer, the higher the stage, the more extensive it is. And Stage IV is the fourth, or highest, stage, signifying that the disease has spread to distant parts of the body. Doctors also analyze other characteristics of each patient's cancer, such as the specific type of cell and how likely it is to run rampant. For Mary Jo's family, the main message was this: Mary Jo's disease was advanced. "I remember thinking, 'Oh wow, here we go. This could be the end,'" Amy said. "I just remember being so upset."

Ironically, just as Mary Jo had been moving to a new home when she was first diagnosed in 1992, the same thing was happening at the time of her 2002 re-diagnosis. Mary Jo had already purchased a one-acre lot in the River's Bend golf course community in Warren County's Hamilton Township, a choice she made after her sister-in-law, Ginny Kuntz, informed her about this newer subdivision. Mary Jo thought the location was perfect in so many ways, Ginny said, recalling Mary Jo saying, "I love to play golf, and it's one exit away from one of my children and two exits away from the other one." Besides being midway between the homes of Spence and Amy, Mary Jo's new custom home was being built on a street with a symbolic name: Sanctuary Lane.

Because of the re-diagnosis, Mary Jo wanted to know whether she would be around to enjoy that house. She asked her doctor a frank, pointed question right after he delivered the awful news: "Will I be around in ten years?"

"The doctor wouldn't say 'yes' for sure," Amy recalled, "but he did say, 'I think so.'"

So, Mary Jo proceeded with finishing the Sanctuary Lane home in River's Bend. The house was such a showplace, *Inspire Cincinnati* magazine featured it in a six-page spread, along with an article that highlighted how Mary Jo fought cancer while the home was under construction. In the article, builder Vinny Terranova said that the Croppers "were on a first-name basis with every subcontractor," and after learning about Mary Jo's cancer, the entire crew became emotionally involved in the project.

Soon after moving to Sanctuary Lane, Mary Jo took on another big project: building a house on Norris Lake in Tennessee. Family friends had introduced the Croppers to Norris Lake, and they fell in love with it. Like the Croppers' other hangout, Lake

The home that Mary Jo had built despite her second bout with cancer. Located in the River's Bend golf course community, this house on Sanctuary Lane was featured in a magazine article.

Cumberland in Kentucky, Norris Lake also is a reservoir. But Norris is about half the size of Cumberland, providing a more intimate setting. Mary Jo selected a site in the area called The Peninsula at Norris Lake.

Also, owning a house there would be easier than maintaining the houseboat on Lake Cumberland. Houseboat ownership comes with seasonal hassles of putting them into and out of storage. "Mom and Dad found themselves working on the houseboat more than enjoying it," said the Croppers' son, Spence. Another advantage: Whereas Cumberland is mostly accessed via marinas, shoreline homes with private boat docks are permitted along Norris Lake and nearby rivers. "Tennessee's rolling green hills protect the peaceful turquoise water of Norris Lake," a description on norrislake.com says.

Building the Norris Lake house was one of the best things Mary Jo ever did. Its tranquil setting rejuvenated her.

"For her, it was a place to unwind; it was her haven away from cancer," Spence said. "There were no doctor's appointments down there." Just relaxation—and sharing wine, games and laughter with people she loved.

Not long after moving into the Norris Lake house, Mary Jo put a four-foot-tall statue of a smiling, furry bear on prominent display. Standing front-and-center, the bear seems to "supervise" visitors while cradling a wooden sign that proclaims a Mary Jo-approved slogan: "Memories Made Here." The bear adds a touch of whimsy to the décor dominated by hardwood, stonework and expansive windows. To set the tone for each gathering, the Croppers and their houseguests dress the bear in various outfits, such as Ohio State apparel during football season or a neon strapless dress, sunhat and pearl necklace for a summer celebration.

Being at Norris Lake allowed Mary Jo to set aside her health problems for the most part. At times, she felt almost like her pre-cancer self again; she just kicked back and had a good time, sometimes with her Hawaii buddies, The Wahines. After one such visit, Talitha Colston wrote Mary Jo a thank-you note in the houseguest book, saying, "There's never been a dull moment when the Wahines are together. It seems fun just follows us everywhere we go. We are truly blessed with such friendship. Thank you for giving us a place to be together and let it all 'hang out.'"

A few times, medical problems disrupted Mary Jo's visits to the lake house. She was forced to make the twenty-five-minute drive to the closest hospital, LaFollette Medical Center. A couple times, Mary Jo found herself in some memorable circumstances there. Once, because Mary Jo was suffering an uncontrollable nosebleed—a side effect of her medication—her son, Spence, took her to the emergency room. As she waited for care, Mary Jo was seated next to a jail inmate wearing an orange jumpsuit, Spence recalled. Another time, Mary Jo went to the ER after she tripped and fell at the Norris Lake golf course. While she was being treated for a cut on her leg, her relatives sat beside a drunk guy who had passed out—with a backdrop of Halloween skeletons and "R.I.P." gravestones on them. "It was the most uncheerful thing you can think of," Mary Jo's sister, Sandy Perry, said. Someone snapped a photo of Mary Jo in a wheelchair with those morbid decorations behind her.

Except for those ER visits, Norris Lake was the place where Mary Jo reconnected with peace. Years later, Mary Jo made a comment that revealed how much she valued her Norris Lake getaways. A bunch of ladies had gathered at the home of Ginny Kuntz, Mary Jo's sister-in-law, to raise funds for Kindervelt, a charity that benefits Cincinnati Children's Hospital Medical Center. Mary Jo spearheaded the Lebanon chapter of that organization, partly in tribute to her father, Ralph Stolle; the hospital had been one of his favorite charities. As an ice-breaking activity, attendees at Ginny's fund-raiser were asked this question: "What would be your dream vacation?"

Marsha Falknor, the woman who had made so many travel arrangements for Mary Jo, was curious: Where on earth would this well-traveled woman most want to visit? Mary Jo answered: "Our house on Norris Lake."

Marsha was stunned—and touched. "I thought, 'Wow, she didn't need a big, fancy trip,'" Marsha said. "All she needed was just the peacefulness of it, the serenity of it—and the together-

Granddaughter Josie and Mimi enjoy a boat ride on Norris Lake in Tennessee.

ness with her family. That was what she needed most at that time in her life."

Meanwhile, another woman who did work for Mary Jo, financial expert Sally Alspaugh, had also become personally attached to her.

In early 2002, as soon as Sally found out that Mary Jo's cancer was back, she knew she needed to give Mary Jo a gift. Not just any gift, but a meaningful one. "Mary Jo's 'love language' was gifts; my 'love language' is gifts," Sally said. "I immediately set out to find a G.I. Jane doll," the newer, female version of the 1960s G.I. Joe military doll. After some searching, Sally found a G.I. Jane. She took it to Mary Jo and told her: "I want you to have this, to symbolize that I want you to fight."

That was already Mary Jo's strong intention, but every little boost helped. Mary Jo was more determined than ever to live as long as she could and to be as happy as possible each day, despite cancer. After her re-diagnosis, "making memories went 'on steroids,'" her son, Spence, said. "Everything was about photos and making memories—just spending time with all of us and other people who were important to her."

In 2003, the year after Mary Jo's cancer recurred, she went on at least two notable trips, one with a huge group of women—and the other, with a small group that included Sally.

Mary Jo was among twenty-five Ohio ladies who went to Las Vegas. That time, Marsha Falknor didn't just plan the trip—she also went on it. Mary Jo introduced Marsha to Rombauer wine during that trip. Mary Jo was so fun-loving, and promoted Rombauer with such passion, it was easy to imagine her stomping grapes to make the wine—just as comedienne Lucille Ball once did in *I Love Lucy*. Mary Jo often watched that 1950s TV show when she was a child.

Now, as an adult, there never was a shortage of laughs when Mary Jo was with her friends. She loved to joke around.

While in Vegas, Mary Jo and about two dozen other women stayed at the Bellagio hotel, known for its spectacular water-fountain show set to music. And each night, the group went to a different show on the Las Vegas Strip, including impressionist Danny Gans, who was known as "The Man of Many Voices," and has since passed away. The women also "oohed" and "ahhed" at O, the water-acrobatics-and-dance performance by the Cirque du Soleil entertainment troupe.

During that same year, Sally Alspaugh organized a trip to Ireland. Three couples went: Mary Jo and Robbie Cropper; Robbie's sister, Ginny, and her husband, Ron Kuntz; and Sally and her husband at the time, Jon Alspaugh.

Flipping through a photo album of that trip, Sally, now known as Sally Finn, smiled as she reminisced about how happy Mary Jo seemed. "She just has this big grin in every picture," Sally said. "It was just a very pleasant trip." The six Ohioans appreciated the pastoral beauty of the Irish countryside and the hospitality they experienced, especially in quaint places where they found food and lodging. "In the fancy hotels, you get a better pillow—but nobody talks to each other," Sally said.

During that trip, all three of the ladies—Mary Jo, Ginny and Sally—bought handcrafted Irish dinnerware by Nicholas Mosse, depicting farmhouses and dairy cows. Sally remembers Mary Jo saying those designs brought to mind her childhood on the SanMarGale farm. Thus, Mary Jo tied a distant memory to her strand of newly minted ones. And, to her, each one was as precious as a genuine pearl.

Many people admired Mary Jo's ability to view life through a lens tinted with sunshine, despite cancer's cloud hovering over her. But two years into her recurrence, a mishap put Mary Jo's coping skills to their most severe test yet.

On December 10, 2004, Mary Jo and Robbie had breakfast at Bob Evans restaurant in Lebanon with their granddaughters,

Josie, then not quite 4 years old, and Sophie, 2. It was a Friday morning, and the girls had spent Thursday night at their Mimi and Pa's Sanctuary Lane home. The four of them were headed back to the girls' home on Judkins Lane. Carved into land that their great-grandpa Stolle had once owned, the street was named after the girls' great-grandma, the former Dorothy Judkins; she had died years before they were born.

The drive to Judkins Lane should have taken only three minutes along State Route 123. But it was a rainy, foggy day. And the family was traveling through an accident-prone area called Alexander's Hill. About halfway through that short trip, around 9:45 a.m., a semi tractor-trailer jackknifed as it rounded an S-curve in the midst of a downhill grade. The truck slid out-of-control on the wet pavement. Then it went left-of-center. And, suddenly, the westbound truck was barreling toward the Croppers' vehicle, head-on.

Robbie was driving a Lexus sedan. He reacted instinctively to save his wife's side of the car from the brunt of the impact with the truck. He turned the steering wheel to his right and ran the Lexus' passenger side into a guardrail, knowing that his side of the vehicle would collide with the truck. After impact, the Lexus whipped around violently.

As it spun, Mary Jo glanced into the back seat toward Josie and Sophie. She was terrified that she might see they were hurt. Instead, Mary Jo saw the strangest thing: a glow surrounding the girls, "as if it were protecting them," Spence said.

Mary Jo would later say she was convinced that angels had intervened to shield the girls from harm. Neither girl suffered even a scratch in the wreck that totaled the Lexus. And Mary Jo told her son: "There wasn't even a piece of glass on them, either."

Dana said: "As your kids grow up, you look back and see times in their lives when the hand of God was on them—and this is one of those times." Police later told the family that, if the Croppers had been driving a car that was less-well-constructed than the Lexus LX sedan, or if Robbie had turned the steering wheel differently, "all four of them would have been killed," Spence said.

Both Robbie and Mary Jo were hurt even though the front airbags deployed. All four of the Croppers were wearing seat belts, a family attorney's record said.

At the time of the crash, Robbie's sister, Ginny Kuntz, was attending a women's Bible study group at the Episcopal Church on Main Street in Lebanon. "I heard an ambulance go by, and I just lifted up a prayer. That's just a habit I've had for years. But then I get home and I hear that Robbie and Mary Jo have been in an accident, and I realized this ambulance had been headed for them."

Right after the wreck, Mary Jo called Spence, who was working in an office five miles away. She also called Dana, who was at home with their newborn, Lily. Mary Jo calmly told each of them: There had been "a bad accident," but the girls were OK. However, Mary Jo told Spence, "Your father's hurt; you need to get here."

Dana enlisted a friend to come take care of the baby. She and Spence hurried to the scene. As soon as Spence got close, he saw police cars blocking the road. He parked his car. He ran past a police officer without saying a word. Then Spence sprinted down Alexander's Hill to reach his kids and his parents. Years later, Spence could still picture everything. The wrecked semi. The mangled car with a shattered windshield. His mother and Josie still sitting in the wreckage. A medic holding Sophie, who had vomited. Other medics swarming around his dad, whose face was covered in blood. Spence later learned the source of the blood was a painful but not life-threatening injury. Robbie had bitten through his own lip during the impact.

As emergency crews tried to get Mary Jo out of the vehicle, she kept saying that she couldn't move her legs. That sounded serious, Spence thought at the time.

Dana also had arrived at the crash site. She rode in an ambulance with Mary Jo and Sophie to Bethesda North Hospital while Spence accompanied Josie and Robbie.

At the hospital, X-rays showed that both of Mary Jo's knee-caps were fractured. Because her cancer had spread to her bones, doctors feared that the injuries might not heal. She started wondering, "Am I ever going to walk again? Is this another 'beginning of the end?'" Spence said. "But bless her heart, she pushed through it."

As for Robbie, he shattered a bone in his lower left leg—and pieces of that bone had scattered internally. By inserting a plate and screws, a surgeon tried to stabilize the bone and encourage it to grow back together. But the bone never healed completely, leaving his legs misaligned, Spence said.

The accident added to increasing concerns about the Alexander's Hill area; Dana and Spence were among citizens who addressed Warren County Commissioners at a meeting four days after the crash. As a result, the county engineer's office later worked with state officials to make safety improvements. They installed new guardrails, cleared trees to improve sight distance and added flashing yellow warning lights. In addition, the speed limit was lowered by 10 mph, to 45 mph. Witnesses to the Cropper wreck had estimated that the semi was traveling close to the 55-mph limit when it went out of control.

For about six weeks after the crash, Robbie and Mary Jo were stuck in wheelchairs to recover from their injuries. Having both of them in wheelchairs at the same time was awkward, to say the least. But the two of them tried to find humor in it, too, Ginny said: "He would say, 'I'm going forward!' She would say, 'I'm going back!' And they both would go, 'Beep, beep, beep!'"

Because Mary Jo's knees needed to remain straight for a while, they were immobilized in braces—and extended in front of her as she sat in the wheelchair. She was quite a sight when Spence wheeled her into a preschool Christmas program within days of the accident. Despite her injuries, Mary Jo was determined to hear her granddaughter, Josie, sing in a group with Ginny's granddaughter. When the kids sang, "We Wish You a Merry Christmas," spectators really got a kick out of Josie's performance. Josie, who turned 4 shortly after the accident, sang with gusto, Ginny recalled. Every time Josie sang the word, "wish," she belted it out with gusto—and further punctuated it by punching her arm in a downward arc. Many Christmases later, re-enacting Josie's technique—or even just describing how cute it was—made Ginny and other relatives chuckle.

As time passed after the accident, Mary Jo's leg braces were gradually adjusted to allow a little more movement, Spence said. Still, she was unable to bear weight on her legs for nearly two months—partly because of the injury itself and partly because doctors were extra-cautious about her bones already being weakened by cancer.

Given that Mary Jo had no choice but to have her legs stick out, Ginny figured she might as well make those legs even more noticeable. So, Ginny went to a Lebanon gift shop, Oh Suzanna, known for its unusual selections, and hunted for "the craziest socks I could buy." Ginny was happy that Mary Jo did seem to enjoy sporting those colorful socks. Tears filled Ginny's eyes, knowing she had done something small that cheered up Mary Jo.

The accident's aftermath presented one of the roughest patches that Robbie and Mary Jo had to overcome during their decades-long history as a couple, Ginny said. "Usually, when he was 'down,' she was 'up'—or the other way around—and they were able to take care of each other," Ginny said. "But this time, they were both 'down.'"

In the midst of all of that turmoil, Mary Jo and Robbie still agreed to host a church retreat at their home.

Mary Jo's son, Spence, said the accident created the second-biggest challenge of his mom's life, outranked only by her cancer battle.

"It was just awful for her watching my dad deteriorate and not being able to take care of him," Spence said, "because she could hardly take care of herself."

At times, normally upbeat Mary Jo did feel overwhelmed. If she had chosen to wallow in self-pity, no one would have faulted her. Instead, Mary Jo redoubled her efforts to help others, even if it just meant she made a phone call or wrote a note. Because she had already discovered this: Altruism was more powerful for her soul than any prescription was for her body.

Less than a year later, just when it seemed she had recovered from the accident, Mary Jo felt like she was knocked down again. Nan Sempsrott, her bestie since childhood, was diagnosed with breast cancer.

Now, in the fall of 2005, these two women, who had shared so many pleasant memories since seventh grade, were now sharing an experience they never would have wished on anyone.

Mary Jo accompanied Nan to the Bethesda North Center for Breast Care. Mary Jo had been diagnosed and treated elsewhere, so she had never visited that facility until she went with Nan.

Mary Jo later wrote that she was "totally impressed" with the care that Nan received there. "From the genuine compassion of the staff to the efficiency of arranging further appointments, everything was handled to help ease the patient's concerns and confusion when you are facing all these decisions," Mary Jo wrote later.

Then, in early 2006, Mary Jo was floored when she learned that another dear friend, her college roommate, Martie Bowden Mehallis, was also diagnosed with breast cancer. And Martie kept hitting roadblocks and delays. Six months passed between the discovery of Martie's lump and her surgery. Martie had no help setting her appointments. She often had to track down her own test results.

Mary Jo was struck by the contrast between Nan's experiences at Bethesda and Martie's experiences in Florida. "The stress she experienced during the six-month period was emotionally debilitating, to say the least, and totally unnecessary," Mary Jo wrote. In contrast, Mary Jo pointed out that Nan's treatment path was much quicker and easier. Only a month elapsed between Nan's original mammogram and her lumpectomy—and the Center staff scheduled all of Nan's appointments, too, Mary Jo noted.

Within a few months, Mary Jo would come to believe that her seeing the "night-and-day" difference between her two friends' experiences had been meant-to-be. Unbeknownst to Mary Jo, around the time of Nan's initial visits, the Bethesda Foundation had approved a fundraising campaign for a new breast center. "The need for expansion was obvious," said Mary Fischer, who was then in charge of major gifts for the Foundation. The existing Center was shoehorned into a corner of Bethesda North on the first floor, with nowhere to grow—"and they were at capacity," Mary said. And Mary was trying to generate $2.5 million for the new Center. But she had a big problem. Because Mary was new to her job, she lacked the personal relationships that could put her in touch with people who were inclined to make major donations.

Friends since seventh grade, Nan Sempsrott and Mary Jo shared so many things—and then both faced breast cancer. Because of Nan, Mary Jo was introduced to the place where a medical facility would later be established in Mary Jo's name.

So, six weeks into her new job, Mary asked members of the foundation's Major Planned Gifts Committee: "I need your help to 'open some doors' for me." She asked members to scan a list of past donors, and to alert her to any names of people who might be receptive to the Breast Center campaign. "And, just as importantly," Mary asked, "please tell me about anyone who isn't on this list and should be."

Sally Alspaugh, the Croppers' financial gal, happened to be at that meeting. Knowing about Mary Jo's personal history, Sally had an "aha!" moment. She thought Mary Jo's name should be on the prospective-donors list. But because of client confidentiality, all Sally could say to Mary Fischer was: "I know someone who may be interested. Let me get back to you."

Sally sensed a near-perfect match between donor and cause. She knew that Mary Jo's father, Ralph Stolle, had a history of charitable giving. And she also knew that Mary Jo's breast cancer had recurred. Against that backdrop, "the connection was obvious," Sally said. Mary Jo almost certainly would want to support efforts to detect, diagnose, treat and study the same disease that she had been fighting. "The model was there for a gift of significance," Sally said, "not only for the community, but also for that family."

After that meeting, Sally met with Robbie and Mary Jo and described the opportunity that had presented itself. As Sally recalls it, Mary Jo simply said, "I'll think about it."

After talking with Robbie, Mary Jo told Sally that she was ready to seriously consider making a contribution. Sally introduced her to Mary Fischer.

Mary's notes say that, on May 15, 2006, she went on a tour of the existing Center with Sally, Mary Jo and two women who made the Center tick: medical director Dr. Susan Weinberg and supervisor Jacqui Appel.

The meeting couldn't have gone any better. "I could just tell there was electricity between Mary Jo and Susan," Sally said. "Susan was talking in a language that resonated with Mary Jo. You could see that Susan dreamed of a more beautiful, more empathetic, more personalized experience for patients." Mary Jo kept nodding in agreement.

The need for a new Center was painfully obvious. Because the existing Center had been cobbled together, it was "almost like a maze," Mary Fischer said. The waiting room was often overflowing; patients were standing in the hallway. "Any prospective donor who took a tour was convinced that there was an immediate need for a new breast center," Mary said. Despite the cramped conditions, the staff "made do," and prided itself on compassionate care, while biding their time, hoping for a new facility.

"There was a sense of urgency," Mary said, "because they were bursting at the seams."

After the tour, discussion continued at a charming restaurant nearby, Ferrari's Little Italy. Mary Fischer remembers listening to Mary Jo share her own history with breast cancer. Mary Jo also described the vastly different recent experiences of her two great friends, Nan and Martie. Mary Jo seemed "so pleasant, so upbeat," Mary Fischer recalled. Mary said she had heard "what a kind and generous person Mary Jo was." Those characteristics shined through, Mary said. So, Mary decided to gently encourage Mary Jo to consider making "a leadership gift"—any monetary contribution in the six-figure range. Making such a suggestion is always a delicate matter.

As the meeting ended, Mary Jo declared: "You've given me a lot to think about."

The next day, Mary Fischer sent a handwritten thank-you note to Mary Jo, along with a packet of information about the Breast Center fundraising campaign. Then Mary just waited to hear from Mary Jo.

Mary Jo looked over the brochure. It described "naming opportunities" for people who made major contributions. Topping the list: "Name the Breast Center, $1,000,000." That one appealed to Mary Jo.

She and Robbie reviewed their finances. They asked Amy and Spence to come to a family meeting. It was important for them to get their children's approval because Mary Jo's intended gift would affect their financial future.

As he recalls, his mom broached the subject without fanfare. She said: "I've got this opportunity to make this donation—and are you guys okay with us doing that?" Spence looked at his father, the financial guru of the family, for a reaction. Robbie replied, "Yes, we can afford to do this." But Mary Jo expressed her concern: "It's a sacrifice for all of you guys if I make this gift." But she viewed this as an opportunity to leave a legacy for the entire family. And, in keeping with her humble profile, Mary Jo suggested that the Center be named not for her, but for the family.

Amy and Spence liked the idea of helping to ease the journey for other breast cancer patients.

Thus, it was settled: a million-dollar contribution from Mary Jo would be headed for the Bethesda Foundation to establish a new Breast Center in the Croppers' name.

After that, Sally remembers getting a call—the call—on her office phone. "Mary Jo was on the line, and she said, real quickly, 'Robbie and I have decided to give a million dollars to the Center.'" Sally exclaimed, "Mary Jo, that's awesome! Is it alright if I tell Bethesda?" Yes, Mary Jo said. Sally said she would then get back with Mary Jo and tell her what the next steps would be.

Sally immediately dialed the phone number for Ed Osofsky, then president and CEO of the Bethesda Foundation. Sally asked whether Ed and other leaders were available for a quick, in-person meeting; her office was only a five-minute drive from Bethesda. When Sally arrived, she said, "Ed, sit down. I have a donor who would like to give one million dollars to the Breast Center!" The reaction was jubilation. "We all jumped up and down and kind of screamed," Sally said.

On that date, July 20, 2006, Mary Jo was unaware that she was committing to the largest single-donor gift that the Bethesda Foundation had received since its inception in 1974. Mary Jo's donation became a pacesetter. In the years that followed, other donors made even bigger contributions to the Foundation.

It took three months to iron out all the details of Mary Jo's gift. On October 26, 2006, Mary Jo signed a three-page agreement pledging installments totaling $1 million for a new Breast Center—one capable of serving up to sixty thousand patients a year, more than double the patient load that the existing Center was handling.

Few of those patients would have any idea who Mary Jo was; large numbers of them would just be getting screening exams and would never face a cancer diagnosis. But all of them would benefit from the new Center. And that, for Mary Jo, is what mattered.

7

Dreamcatchers

Finally, it was happening: Dr. Susan Weinberg's decade-old dream was about to come true, thanks to a woman she hardly knew, Mary Jo Cropper.

After learning that Mary Jo had committed to her generous donation in the summer of 2006, Dr. Weinberg almost had to pinch herself to make sure that this was real: a new breast care center would be established at Bethesda—and it would serve *thirty thousand more patients* with state-of-the-art equipment and programs. The original center inside Bethesda North Hospital was already seeing about thirty thousand people; by doubling the number of patients it could handle, the new Center was poised to save many more lives.

For years, Dr. Weinberg and members of the breast center's staff had seen the need for care was rising. Four counties—Butler, Clermont, Hamilton and Warren—make up Bethesda's service area. In that four-county region, the need for breast care was climbing about 2 percent a year, based on increases in the 35-and-up female population. In just four years, there were thirty thousand more women in that age range, many of whom would be recommended for annual mammograms.

At the same time, Hamilton County, Ohio, where Bethesda is located, was seeing breast cancer rates outpacing state and national ones. Per 100,000 Hamilton County women, 144 would develop breast cancer—14 more cases than Ohio statewide and seven more than the national rate. Hamilton County women were also dying more often from breast cancer. Dr. Weinberg presented those facts and figures during a 2006 fundraising campaign, citing the Ohio Department of Health and the National Cancer Institute.

At center, Dr. Susan Weinberg and her friend, Mary Jo Cropper, and at rear, hospital executive Sher McClanahan, are surrounded by "Girls on the Run." That was one of many groups that contributed to the fundraising campaign for the Mary Jo Cropper Family Center for Breast Care.

Yet the original Bethesda North Center for Breast Care had no room for expansion to keep pace with the growing population's needs.

When that center first opened its doors in December 1995, "we had only about three thousand square feet under a stairwell," Dr. Weinberg said. "And it was chopped up into small areas. But it was better than nothing."

Despite the lack of space, Dr. Weinberg said she was given this mission as founder and medical director of the center: "We want you to do it all, and we want you to do it seamlessly." And, Dr. Weinberg said, there was no comprehensive breast care program anywhere in Bethesda's service area at that time. She solicited suggestions from patients, staff, specialists and primary care doctors. She also researched "best practices" across the nation.

As a result, the center pioneered the Cincinnati region's first Breast Panel, Dr. Weinberg said. The Panel included more than a dozen medical professionals who would meet weekly to review newly diagnosed cancer cases. The panelists would then work together to customize recommendations for each patient. That process was remarkably beneficial to doctors and patients alike, said Dr. Ted Jones. Now retired, Dr. Jones was Bethesda's first breast surgeon. Typically, when patients were told they had breast cancer, "they and their families would get into a whirlpool of worry," he said. Then they would seek multiple opinions about how to proceed—and those opinions would often conflict, adding to anxiety, confusion and delays. But after Dr. Weinberg instituted the Breast Panel, Dr. Jones was able to tell patients: "Here's what your situation is, and this is the consensus of seventeen or eighteen opinions." Thus, patients—and their physicians—had a lot more confidence in the diagnoses and treatment plans, Dr. Jones said.

While launching such initiatives, Dr. Weinberg and her staff were begging for more room. But Bethesda was busy with corporate reorganization. In 1995, the same year the center began, Bethesda and Good Samaritan hospitals merged to form the TriHealth system. And economic conditions were difficult for healthcare systems across the nation then. Those were among the reasons why plans for a new breast center kept being pushed to the back burner.

Still, Dr. Weinberg was undaunted. The center expanded into some adjacent spaces and gained another couple thousand square feet.

And behind the scenes, Dr. Weinberg was lining up support for the new Center. "I needed buy-in from the physician community that referred to us," she said. She networked with primary care doctors, general surgeons, plastic surgeons and oncologists (cancer specialists), as well as obstetrics and gynecology doctors.

All the while, she pushed for other improvements at the existing center—and succeeded, despite the limited space.

In 2001, with the help of a Fifth Third Bank grant, the original center installed one of the Cincinnati area's first computer-assisted systems for breast cancer detection. The computer would double-check radiologists' work, improving detection rates by 5 percent to 15 percent, Dr. Weinberg said.

In 2002, the breast center began enrolling patients in clinical trials—research studies of new treatment methods. The center also established the region's first program to give extra attention to patients who were considered high risk for developing breast cancer.

And the original center had established an excellent track record for detecting breast cancer early. Cancer classifications range from Stage I through Stage IV. The higher the stage, the more the disease has progressed. During a 2006 presentation, Dr. Weinberg said it was then considered a "best practice" to detect 75 percent of cases at Stage II or earlier; the Bethesda center exceeded that mark, discovering 90 percent of new cases during those earlier stages. And that meant those patients had a better chance of surviving at least five years.

Dr. Weinberg's presentation also depicted the uncomfortable circumstances that patients were facing in the original center. A photograph of a waiting area shows only eight chairs, all of which were filled—and that was on a less-busy day, Dr. Weinberg said. Seven of the women were wearing hospital gowns as they apparently waited for mammograms—definitely not an ideal situation. Dr. Weinberg desperately wanted shorter wait times and more privacy for those patients.

During its first year, the original center handled ten thousand mammograms; hospital officials estimated that the center would reach capacity in about a dozen years. Instead, the breast center was "maxed-out" in half that time: about six years. By 2002, it was serving more than twenty-seven thousand patients. The number of patients stayed around that level for the next four years because the center just couldn't handle any more appointments, Dr. Weinberg said. Patients who couldn't be served at the center may have sought appointments elsewhere—or, worse yet, may have skipped examinations altogether.

Moving to a new location, largely with Mary Jo's financial help, was essential.

Even after getting Mary Jo's million-dollar commitment, Dr. Weinberg knew that an all-hands-on-deck effort would be needed. "You can't do anything like this by yourself; you need everybody to help," Dr. Weinberg said.

First, another $1.5 million was needed to reach the fundraising goal for the new Center. Then, Dr. Weinberg, her staff and many other people would need to take dozens of steps to make the Center materialize.

Employees at the existing center—and throughout the Tri-Health system—rallied. During the three-year fundraising campaign, about sixteen hundred TriHealth workers made contributions totaling a half-million dollars, Mary Fischer said. "That was an unprecedented level of employee giving, from what I understand," she said. "It was very humbling to know that our employees were that vested in the campaign."

Spearheaded by supervisor Jacqui Appel, the existing center's staff organized creative fundraisers, such as parties with end-of-summer, Halloween and Cincinnati Bengals themes. Two benefit dances raked in a total of thirty-four thousand dollars. The group sold baked goods, cookbooks and breast cancer awareness T-shirts with witty catchphrases such as, "Help save 'second base'—it's worth it!"

News of Mary Jo's gift made the breast center's employees feel even more motivated to do their part, Jacqui said. "It was going to be 'our' Center, to make things better for our patients, and we just wanted to be part of it," she said. "Mary Jo and her initial gift were just so inspirational."

As often happens with fundraising, other major donors came forward after Mary Jo's big donation was secured. Claire B. Phillips—a pilot for the family-owned Phillips Supply Company in Cincinnati—signed over her entire house to the Bethesda Foundation. In doing so, Ms. Phillips earmarked a six-figure donation for the new Center; its lobby was named after her. She has since passed away.

Other substantial gifts came from many sources, including Cincinnati-area philanthropist Harold Thomas and his now-deceased wife, Margret. Another came from the Charlotte R. Schmidlapp Fund at Fifth Third Bank: a two-hundred-thousand-dollar matching gift for the employee-giving campaign.

An array of smaller donations to the new Center came from local businesses, individuals and groups—totaling $5 million, more than double the original fundraising goal, Mary Fischer said. People saw the Center as something that was needed—and many people also had a soft spot for the cause because "almost everyone seems to know someone who has had breast cancer," Mary said.

Without realizing it, Mary Jo, Dr. Weinberg, the original center's staff and so many other supporters all had dreamt the same vision—separately. Together, they moved forward to make it a reality.

Even before any plans for the new Center were drawn up, Mary Jo and Dr. Weinberg had begun collaborating on how to make patients' experiences less stressful.

"Mary Jo was a woman looking for a program and a system because she did not have that. She had to go here, there and everywhere to get her care," Dr. Weinberg said. "She found that undesirable—and she was absolutely right."

Mary Jo had already visited the existing center with her lifelong friend, Nan Sempsrott; she had seen the superior care Nan received as a newly diagnosed cancer patient, despite the cramped conditions.

When Mary Jo went on her official tour of the original center in 2006, Dr. Weinberg tried to help her imagine what it could become. "Mary Jo came to the little bitty breast center, and I said, 'This doesn't seem like much, but this is the vision for what we want to do,'" Dr. Weinberg said. "And she 'got it.' She totally understood it." The goal was to house many related services for patients in the same building, making it a so-called "one-stop shop" as much as possible.

A few months after that tour with Dr. Weinberg, Mary Jo wrote a note telling Mary Fischer: "From the moment I stepped into the center, I knew I'd found a place where I could possibly make a difference.... I'm privileged to participate in this much-needed expansion."

The breast center was already providing some leading-edge services at the time—notably the Breast Panel case reviews plus on-site radiologists to give same-day diagnoses to patients. Dr. Weinberg pictured many other improvements in equipment, personnel and patient care. She saw a need for a mobile mammography van to serve women who might have a hard time getting to the Bethesda breast center. And she wanted the new Center to serve as a central hub for several satellite breast centers.

Mary Jo "clicked" with what Dr. Weinberg was saying. "Mary Jo understood the disease. She understood the demands of the disease and how to best meet the needs of the patient," Dr. Weinberg said. "She knew how important it was that the patient's needs be met in a prompt, effective fashion. She discovered how important it was to be 'cutting-edge.' To meet a layperson who 'got it' like that was just exceptional."

Dr. Weinberg introduced Mary Jo to a relatively new concept that she wanted to formally implement: nurse navigators, who are specially trained to guide newly diagnosed cancer patients. They answer patients' questions, offer reassurance and help them through the complex maze of treatments, testing, counseling and other services. The goal is "survivorship," the post-treatment period that, hopefully, would remain cancer-free for the rest of the patient's life. Every step of the way, the nurse navigator keeps the patient informed and listens to concerns.

That idea stood out to Mary Jo. And, as it turned out, when Mary Jo toured the original center, "she was talking to some of the people who later became navigators," Dr. Weinberg said.

One of the Bethesda center's longest-serving employees, Tina German, was among those who later became a navigator.

Nurse Tina German discusses the evolution of breast care at Bethesda North Hospital, where she has worked since 1980. She worked at the Bethesda North Center for Breast Care beginning in 1997, then went on to work at the Cropper Center after it opened in 2009.

Tina only met Mary Jo a few times in passing, but Mary Jo left this impression: "She was so-down-to-earth, you felt like you could just call her and ask her to go have coffee or lunch."

Tina has seen remarkable changes since she first started working at Bethesda in 1980. Back then, the hospital consisted of "one little tower;" by 2020, six buildings were bustling with activity on the hospital's campus in Montgomery, Ohio. One of them houses the Mary Jo Cropper Family Center for Breast Care.

There was no such facility when Tina first started working at the hospital forty years ago. In fact, back then, "women did not talk about their breasts," she said. Nor did people talk much about cancer of any kind, especially not cancers that attacked female-specific areas: the breast, ovaries or uterus. Those cancers seemed too "personal" to discuss. Some people still feel uncomfortable discussing such topics, Tina said.

Another shift: the trend toward preventive medicine and early detection. "In the past, you didn't go to the doctor unless you were really sick," Tina said. As a result, "cancer was pretty much untreatable by the time it was discovered," she said. "Now, people with cancer are living longer," thanks to improved treatment regimens and screening exams that can find cancer even when a person notices no symptoms.

When Dr. Weinberg launched the original center, it was such a new concept that there was no niche for it in the hospital organizational structure; the breast center initially was placed under an unrelated department, cardiology, Tina said.

At the time Tina started working at the original center in 1997, she remembers it consisted of little more than "four chairs and a few examination rooms." Procedures and equipment from that time now seem primitive.

After a woman had a mammogram, technologists would go into a darkroom and develop X-ray images in big tubs filled with chemical solutions. The developed films were large—about 11 inches wide and 17 inches long. Dr. Weinberg, who is a radiologist, would review the X-ray images. If any tissue samples had been obtained, a pathologist would look at those under a microscope. Then a surgeon would review the findings from Dr.

Weinberg and the pathologist. All of that information would go to the Breast Panel for discussion.

Since then, digital images have replaced the time-consuming film-developing method, and the Breast Panel expanded to include professionals in many other disciplines: genetics, nursing, oncology, research and plastic surgery.

Testing also became less invasive. Needles now can be used to extract samples of abnormal-looking areas. "In the past, if a lump looked suspicious, they would just cut it out," Tina said.

Another change: the new Center would have an expanded staff and a formal nurse navigator program. At the original breast center, the only full-time nurse, Glenna Pouliotte, jumped in and performed the functions of a nurse navigator before the program was formally established—and the care Glenna extended to Mary Jo's friend, Nan, caught Mary Jo's attention. "Without Glenna and her personal attention to our breast cancer patients including Nan, we may have not been blessed with Mary Jo's incredible gift," Dr. Weinberg said.

For Mary Jo, those navigators would be among the most important people in the new Center. "Mary Jo really wanted navigation as part of our program," Tina said.

Tina and her co-workers set out to make Mary Jo proud of their work—and not just because she was the lady whose name would be on the building. Just as Mary Jo had inspired her students to please her when she was a teacher, now she was evoking the same response from the Center's employees. She greeted them warmly. "She was always friendly, always smiling," Tina said. The staff admired Mary Jo's altruistic spirit and her upbeat presence despite her struggles with cancer.

"We knew that a lot of these services weren't available to her when she first had to deal with her cancer," Tina said. "That touched all of us, that she wanted to give this gift to other women so they would have it better than she did."

The staff also knew that having a larger space with more equipment would help them to serve more patients with improved efficiency, Tina said.

Tina and other nurses had only a few interactions with Mary Jo, but each one was meaningful. "We could tell that she knew we weren't just fluff and smiles and hugs," Tina said. "She knew we were smart and educated, and she wanted us to be able to guide those patients on their journey to survivorship."

And then there was this powerful motivator, Tina said: "We knew that she was counting on us to make this place successful."

Another veteran employee, Billie Burrus, also would assume an important position in the new Center.

Dr. Weinberg hired Billie as a mammography technologist in 1995, several years after Billie had started a breast center in Charleston, Illinois. Billie moved back to her hometown of Cincinnati and got the job at Bethesda.

Like Tina, Billie can describe outmoded methods that were once used in her field.

Doctors have been using X-rays since the late 1800s to see things inside their patients' bodies. And the first use of X-rays for breast exams dates to around 1913. Decades ago, some technologists actually used some surprising objects—cardboard and a balloon—in an attempt to flatten the breast tissue, thus revealing more detail. Billie learned that method during her training in the 1970s. Now she shakes her head and says, "I don't know what we even saw back then." In addition, old mammography exposed patients to potentially harmful higher doses of X-rays. Now high-tech machines are used to compress the breast and to make images with computers and low-dose X-rays. Thus, today's mammograms provide more comfort and safety for the patient, along with better-quality images for physicians to review.

When Dr. Weinberg hired Billie, Bethesda's first breast center had two rooms for mammography, four dressing rooms and a darkroom for processing mammography films. Billie remembers Dr. Weinberg telling her, "Now, Billie, we're only here temporarily. We're only going to be here a few months." Fourteen years later, the new Center would have eight examination rooms, five mammography rooms and three rooms where ultrasound is used for specialized breast exams. In addition, the Center provided space for the Breast Panel and other large meetings, plus offices for four surgeons whose work is dedicated solely to breast procedures.

Despite its deficiencies, the first Bethesda breast center still saw a number of success stories—one of which is particularly memorable for Billie.

During the late 1990s, a woman in her late 20s was in her first trimester of pregnancy when she found a lump in her breast. She needed a mammogram. So, technologists shielded her pregnant belly from the radiation, and additional tests were done. The result: cancer.

As a result, the young woman needed chemotherapy drugs, which might have harmed the developing baby. "She had the option of aborting. But she didn't do that. And she had a healthy baby boy eight months later," Billie said. "Miracles like this do happen."

That story illustrates the fact that breast cancer isn't limited to middle-aged women; it can be found in young women, too. It also shows that positive outcomes are sometimes possible even when circumstances are complicated, Billie said.

Billie, who would also play an important part in the Cropper Center, said that, as she and other staff members prepared to move to their new quarters, everyone had the same attitude: "We were so excited that we could serve more women, serve them better, and hopefully make an impact on breast cancer survival. That was our dream, our goal."

As plans for the new Center shifted into high gear, Mary Jo was in more frequent contact with Mary Fischer and Dr. Weinberg—both of whom developed an abiding affection for Mary Jo. To them, she was more than the Center's biggest benefactor. She was a lovely human being. And they enjoyed getting to know her.

They couldn't help but love Mary Jo. This was a woman who was such a pleasure to be around. And she sent handwritten thank-you notes for *everything*, it seemed.

"Thank you for 'keeping me company' yesterday," Mary Jo wrote to Mary Fischer on August 8, 2006. Mary Jo had gone to the hospital for a scan, an imaging test that showed whether her cancer had spread further. "Scan days are probably one of my most dreaded," Mary Jo wrote, "but you helped the time go by and my mind not to dwell." Her son, Spence, had accompanied Mary Jo to the hospital, and she told Mary: "As you saw, Spence is just as excited about 'the gift' as I am."

In other notes, Mary Jo repeatedly thanked Mary for feeding her addiction to "Turtles," the gooey pecan-and-caramel chocolates that resemble turtles. Mary Jo found those candies so irresistible, "I literally cannot walk past them," she once wrote. Mary Jo even confessed: She sometimes stashed away Turtles in a secret spot where no one else could find them. Mary Jo, a woman known for sharing so much, apparently drew the line there: Those Turtles were *hers*, thank you.

Between communiques with Mary Fischer, Mary Jo kept in touch with Dr. Weinberg. They would talk about the Center, about her cancer and about life in general. Although Dr. Weinberg exudes professionalism and intelligence, she also comes across as compassionate. Those qualities synched with Mary Jo's, said Regina Eaton, Dr. Weinberg's administrative assistant.

Regina, who retired in 2017, had been a Bethesda employee for 28 years. During that time, she got to know Dr. Weinberg well. Regina admired Dr. Weinberg "because she had a 'never-hold-me-back' mentality; it was a 'push-forward' mentality." Regina, who often fielded phone calls from Mary Jo, sensed a similar quality in her. "She had this very mild, quiet little voice when I talked to her on the phone. Yet she was the type of lady who seemed like she could move mountains," Regina said. "She would get things done."

Regina saw Mary Jo and Dr. Weinberg as a dynamic duo. "You put those two ladies together and you've got a power-house," she said.

Dr. Weinberg and many other people attended a flurry of meetings about the new Center. She and Jamie Easterling, who was then manager of Bethesda's radiology department, started taking trips to other breast centers, along with the original center's supervisor, Jacqui Appel. They looked at equipment and brainstormed ideas. "We wanted to make sure that the new Center had the best equipment and that it did not look like and feel like a hospital," Jamie said.

Another key player in the Center was Dr. Ching Ho—Tri-Health's first female surgeon dedicated to breast surgery, Jamie said. That was important because female breast patients often had said they would prefer a female surgeon. Eventually, the Center would have four surgeons focused solely on breast procedures. But Dr. Ho led the way, Jamie said, giving momentum to the Center proposal. Dr. Ho had done breast surgeries at Bethesda North since 1989 but also worked at other hospitals. Dr. Weinberg lured her to work exclusively at the Bethesda center as plans were being finalized. She became co-director of the new Center alongside Susan Weinberg.

Jamie listed the main ingredients in the recipe for the Cropper Center's completion: "Susan's vision, Mary Jo's generosity, and Ching Ho's specialty. And Jacqui was the boots-on-the-ground person who made this happen."

Besides being the biggest single financial contributor to the Center, Mary Jo also was involved in some of the planning and design. Dr. Weinberg remembers Mary Jo distinctly expressing her wishes: "I just want people to feel good when they come in there. I want it to be inviting." One of the few design elements that Mary Jo insisted upon: "No dark colors—too depressing. And no stark white—too clinical. She did not want that," Dr. Weinberg recalled. Those preferences were conveyed loud and clear to the interior designer and to the architect, Dr. Weinberg said.

As time went on, the relationship between Mary Jo and Dr. Weinberg changed. Although their passion for women's healthcare drew them together, they had so much more in common, they learned.

They loved the same wines. Especially Rombauer chardonnay.

They loved the same books and movies.

They both believed in expressing gratitude the old-fashioned way, via handwritten notes.

And the list could go on.

"I cannot say enough good things about Mary Jo," Dr. Weinberg said. "This woman was just so personable. She never failed to ask me about my children and grandchildren; the other person always mattered to her." That trait shined through as Mary Jo continued to help refine plans for the new Center. "If she would see anything that would make a patient's visit less uncomfortable, she would do it," Dr. Weinberg said.

At times, Mary Jo and Dr. Weinberg played different roles. Sometimes Mary Jo was acting as the influential patron of the biggest project that Dr. Weinberg had ever undertaken. Other times, Mary Jo was a cancer patient who trusted the expertise of the woman in the white doctor's coat, a National Merit Scholar who graduated summa cum laude and went on to a distinguished medical career: Dr. Susan Weinberg.

She was the doctor who stubbornly hung onto a dream that circumstances had threatened to squelch. And she had powerfully bonded with the cancer patient and former schoolteacher who helped her catch that dream.

So, in time, Dr. Susan Weinberg became just "Susan"—Mary Jo's trusted friend.

8

A Masterpiece Materializes

As he prepared to address the crowd at TriHealth's newest building, John Prout was harboring a secret.

This new facility was extra-meaningful for John as a person, not just as a hospital CEO. As he stood in the shiny new Mary Jo Cropper Family Center for Breast Care, a painful memory flooded his heart. Three decades earlier, his sister, Peggy, had died of breast cancer—and she, like Mary Jo, had been a teacher.

When he welcomed the new Center on Bethesda North Hospital's campus in Montgomery, Ohio, John also was aware of another uncanny parallel between his present and his past. In 1979, at the time of his sister's death, John was working at a hospital in St. Louis, Missouri—and it, too, was named Bethesda.

Back then, a relative had called John, urging him to go see Peggy, who lived near Cleveland, Ohio. John had been told that Peggy was ill, but he had no idea how sick she was. He came as soon as he could—and the day after John visited Peggy, she passed away. "The family lore is that she chose when to die," John said, "and she was waiting to see me." He was the last family member to arrive by her side.

John was stunned. Although Peggy had a previous bout with cervical cancer, "she kept it to herself" when she was diagnosed with breast cancer, John said. Perhaps she was trying to shield her young child from worrying about her, John said, "but only she knows why she wanted to go through it alone."

Fast-forward to September 23, 2009. John was heralding the Grand Opening of the Bethesda North Outpatient Imaging Center, where the new Cropper Center occupied the second floor. Located at 10494 Montgomery Road, the former home of the

The mood was uplifting when Mary Jo Cropper, third from left, joined other major donors and hospital leaders at the Grand Opening of the Center bearing her name. She is pictured with Sher McClanahan, Bethesda North Chief Operating Officer; major donor Claire B. Phillips; TriHealth President John Prout; major donor Harold M. Thomas; and Dr. Susan Weinberg, co-founder of the Center.

Cincinnati Eye Institute had undergone an extensive redesign. Two big firms, HDR architects and Turner Construction, gave the old building a modern makeover. Bethesda invested $24.5 million for the entire project, including $5 million from the Center's wildly successful fundraising campaign.

Now, after three years of securing funds and putting together plans, about two hundred people had gathered to applaud the project's completion. "As ribbon-cuttings go, it was more cele-bratory—and more personal," John Prout recalled, "because it involved people who had been affected by breast cancer, includ-ing me." But John kept that fact private as he spoke that day.

A decade later, during an interview for this book, John re-vealed that he had held Peggy's memory close while he inaugu-rated the beautiful new Center—one dedicated to ensuring that women would not travel their breast cancer journeys alone, as his sister had. And that was something special to behold.

"You could *see* the energy in the room," John recalled. "Ev-eryone who was there loved the vision and knew it was the right thing for the patient."

The building had opened for use on August 3, 2009, six weeks prior to the Grand Opening. Since then, ten thousand patients had taken advantage of services in the Cropper Center and in the rest of the building, John said. "And from the very first day, patients have complimented us on how much easier it is to get in and out, and on how welcoming the building is," John remarked during the ceremony.

Another speaker, John Brooks, president of the Bethesda Foundation trustees, said, "If you blindfolded someone and brought them into this building, then asked them to tell you what it was, I don't think anyone would say, 'It's a medical building.' Simply by making the surroundings less clinical and more welcoming, we are improving the patient experience, reducing stress and anxiety."

That was exactly the effect Mary Jo had hoped to create at the Center.

On Grand Opening night, the sky was cloudy, and the sun was almost setting. Even under those conditions, natural light from the floor-to-ceiling windows filled the two-story lobby. And the décor, dominated by light tan and accented with sage, silver and chocolate, created a feeling of comfort. Framed works of art added cheery splashes of color.

Mary Jo couldn't have been more pleased with how the Center had taken shape.

But when John Prout geared up to thank Mary Jo for her contribution, she was a shrinking violet.

Even though *her* million-dollar donation was a linchpin for this building and even though *her* name was displayed above the entryway, Mary Jo had no desire for the attention. In fact, naming the building had been subject to some debate.

"We could hardly get Mary Jo to put her name on the Center. And we kept saying, 'Mary Jo, *you* did this. You're the lady who made this happen,'" Susan Weinberg said. "She was just so unassuming and so willing to help everybody else."

Mary Jo was so reluctant to have the Center named after her, she acquiesced only after the word "family" was added to the title. Thus, she reasoned, her loved ones were being honored along with her.

Now, at the Grand Opening, Mary Jo made herself scarce, almost as if she didn't expect to receive public accolades. "I had to go find her," her good friend, Martie Mehallis, said. "She was upstairs, and I had to *drag* her down there." The staircase leading from the second floor was shaped in a loop, modeled after an "awareness ribbon." People wear those in various colors to symbolize various causes, including pink for breast cancer. But there was no sign of pink in the décor at the Cropper Center, just the neutral palette that Mary Jo found soothing.

Descending to the first-floor lobby, Mary Jo, as usual, made an impression without saying a word. "I remember she looked so beautiful that night," said Marsha Falknor, the travel agent who became Mary Jo's friend. "She was wearing a white silky blouse with a fluffy collar—and she just beamed."

TriHealth President John Prout said he wanted to recognize a remarkable woman whose contribution "would improve the health of women in this community for generations to come." As he said Mary Jo's name and gestured toward her, someone behind Marsha muttered, "*That's* Mary Jo? Look how young she is!" Marsha said, adding, "I think maybe they were expecting some old lady." At that point, Mary Jo was 68. And there were few, if any signs, of the toll that cancer—and treatments—had taken on her body. Onlookers didn't know that Mary Jo's long black skirt concealed unsightly blotches that chemotherapy had left on her legs. Such an apparel choice was often a necessity for Mary Jo. But this time, it was a silent testimonial: She refused to allow anything to mar this special day, a celebration of hope for untold numbers of patients, possibly even her own relatives and friends.

As John concluded his four-minute speech, family, friends and total strangers applauded for Mary Jo and for the other major donors. "Everybody was in tears," Marsha said.

Many people expected the Center's namesake to make a few remarks. However, those who knew Mary Jo best didn't have that expectation. They knew she was still averse to public speaking. Mary Jo called upon her son, Spence, to fulfill that duty. He was a bundle of nerves. Mostly, Spence was afraid he would become too overcome with emotion to finish. Spence knew he would lose all sense of composure if he looked at his mom. He averted his gaze and dove into the speech.

Spence elicited some chuckles when he quipped: "Mom used her power of motherly persuasion and '*suggested*' that I speak—then proceeded to 'suggest' what I would say."

The mood turned more serious as Spence continued, "I apologize to her now for going 'off-script' briefly." Then, to Mary Jo's surprise, Spence summed up her personal story. "Through her ongoing, seventeen-year-plus battle with the disease, Mom's selfless compassion for others, especially other cancer survivors, has been an inspiration to me, to our family, and to everyone who knows her," he said. "Time after time, Mom has forsaken her own concerns for others in need."

When Mary Jo's path intersected with Dr. Susan Weinberg's, "we truly believe it was not a 'coincidence,' but a 'GOD-incidence,'" Spence said. The ingredients that culminated in the new Center "were all in God's plans," Spence said, a belief that his mother had expressed many times.

One of those times was in 2007. In preparation for a fundraiser where the name of the Center would be revealed, Mary Jo wrote a summary of events that led to her "naming-rights" donation. Mary Jo wrote that God had placed her "where she was supposed to be" when she visited the small original center with her friend, Nan Sempsrott, and saw the quality care she received in September 2005. Mary Jo said she believed God had "blessed her with this opportunity." The new Center would provide "comprehensive and compassionate care"—which is what patients need so they can survive breast cancer, she wrote. It's also what they should *expect*, Mary Jo said.

Now, more than two years after Mary Jo wrote those words, the future that Susan Weinberg and Mary Jo had envisioned was materializing before their eyes at the 2009 Grand Opening. Spence told the crowd that the Cropper family played only "a small part" in establishing the Center. "It was truly Dr. Weinberg's persistence to see this vision become a reality," he said, "along with the selfless contributions and dedication of the staff."

The Center employees were touched by Spence's remarks, and by Mary Jo's thoughtful gestures. Before the event, she had sent a congratulatory, fall-themed flower arrangement to the staff, which was on prominent display during the Grand Opening. Thanking her for the flowers, Center Supervisor Jacqui Appel emailed Mary Jo and said: "You have to be one of the most thoughtful individuals I've been blessed to know." At the Grand Opening reception, Mary Jo also had an impact when she spoke individually with Billie Burrus and other Center employees. "One of the things she said to us was: 'This is for you and the women that you serve. *Thank you* for the work that you do,'" Billie recalled.

To close his speech, Spence quoted Proverbs 13:12, "Hope deferred makes the heart sick; but when hopes are realized at last, there is life and joy." Then he said the Grand Opening was joyful because the Center had transformed from a hope into a reality—and it was creating "a brighter future for women and men facing this disease, which was also once just a hope."

Spence's remarks left his mother so verklempt, she emailed Jacqui the next day and said, "I'm still trying to recover from Spence's speech, which I hadn't expected."

Mary Jo also told Jacqui: "Last evening was wonderful, and I'm ever so proud of the Center. I've been blessed to be a part of it."

Between the time that Mary Jo pledged her financial gift to the Center and its dedication, three years had elapsed. During that span, Mary Jo's life experiences had fluctuated more than the altitude of a warplane in a firefight.

By then she had accepted that cancer would be her constant unwelcome companion. Mary Jo braced for more turbulence—whether she had both feet on the ground and was confronting her cancer, or whether she was airborne and flying to yet another incredible destination with her loved ones.

From 2006–09, as the Center's plans progressed, Mary Jo's calendar was filled with discussions about the Center, fundraisers, cancer treatments, medical tests, family functions, volunteer activities and her own informal "cancer outreach" program—visiting, calling and writing to other cancer patients.

Sometimes, those patients helped Mary Jo as much as she helped them. One patient who fell into that category was Karen Wellington. A married mother of two, Karen had been diagnosed with breast cancer when she was just 30 years old. She and Mary Jo met because they both went to the same oncologist, Dr. Robert Cody at Cincinnati Hematology-Oncology. Karen and Mary Jo hit it off; they were both Ohio State University grads and both maintained an upbeat attitude while battling cancer. Mary Jo admired Karen for staying so active. Karen would go play tennis and then go get her chemo treatments while still wearing her tennis skirt.

When Karen died in 2007, she was just 40—and her death took some wind out of Mary Jo's sails. "It took a lot out of her, watching someone so young, with such a zest for life, to pass away at a such a young age," Mary Jo's son, Spence, said.

He remembers how sad his mother was after attending Karen's funeral—but her spirits lifted when she found ways to help keep Karen's memory alive.

After Karen passed away, Mary Jo went to watch Karen's children, Angeline and Robby, play soccer—even though Mary Jo did not particularly enjoy that sport. Her show of support for Karen's children was an act of kindness that Mary Fischer, of the Bethesda Foundation, learned about years later. "This was another story we didn't know about Mary Jo because she didn't tell people she was doing this," Mary said. "She just did it."

Karen's husband, Kent, remembers hanging out with Mary Jo on a crisp fall day, not a cloud in the sky, as Angeline was playing. Because Mary Jo's Buckeyes were also playing that day, she was "decked out in scarlet and grey," Kent said. Kent and Mary Jo sat side-by-side in fold-up chairs at midfield. "She was super vibrant and alive," Kent said. He hangs onto that fond memory.

Right after Karen died, Kent started an organization that sends breast cancer patients and their families on dream vacations, the Karen Wellington Foundation for LIVING with Breast Cancer. Mary Jo attended many events on behalf of the foundation and was very supportive of its mission, Kent said. By 2020, the foundation had sponsored eight hundred getaways, and was operating four chapters in Ohio plus several others in multiple states.

Mary Jo supported the foundation because she understood firsthand how vital it is for cancer patients to get a change of scenery and spend time with loved ones. Between all of her volunteer activities, Mary Jo continued to squeeze in as many memorable trips as she could.

Even though Mary Jo had taken airplane rides more often than some people take road trips, she was actually somewhat antsy about air travel. Her uneasiness probably stemmed from a rough ride aboard her father's private airplane in the mid-1970s. Amy recounts the incident, based on her mother's description: Amy was with her mother, brother and Grandpa Stolle. They were on a flight bound for Grandpa's second home in Fort Myers, Florida. The weather had turned foul, and strong winds were buffeting the small plane. At first, the movement just caused queasy stomachs. But it became so extreme that, "at one point, our heads were hitting the ceiling," Amy said.

The pilot wanted to land. But Grandpa Stolle, being goal-oriented as always, was determined to reach his intended destination. Mary Jo was scared. To soothe her anxiety, her dad told her: "Go ahead and have a cigarette or a glass of wine."

The pilot did end up landing short of Fort Myers. The plane touched down safely in Huntsville, Alabama, before resuming the trip later. Afterward, the pilot either quit or was fired.

There may have been more than one such incident, considering that several of the Stolles were nervous fliers. Mary Jo and her travel companions typically would visit an airport bar for a few soothing swigs of wine or mixed drinks before boarding flights.

The Cincinnati airport, which is actually located in Kentucky, used to have a bar in Terminal 3. That was Mary Jo's pre-flight headquarters. She would always have a drink before she flew, just to relax. On one occasion, an entire group of ladies drank Bloody Marys at that bar with Mary Jo. No one seemed to care that it was a 9 a.m. flight, still breakfast time for most people.

Marsha can remember Mary Jo canceling only two flights. One was in the fall of 2001, when many Americans were afraid to fly. That September 11, terrorists had hijacked airplanes and intentionally crashed them into the World Trade Center's Twin Towers in New York City, killing thousands. Mary Jo's other flight cancellation was in July 2007. She and her husband, Robbie, were supposed to go to Maui, Hawaii. But Mary Jo was afraid that being under airplane-cabin pressure for a long flight—a total of at least ten hours in the air—would set off the nosebleeds that her cancer medication caused. During this time in her life, she preferred shorter trips to places such as Kiawah Island, South Carolina, reachable by a one-hour flight. And it wasn't too difficult to make the five-hour drive to her house on Norris Lake, Tennessee. That's where the Croppers ended up going after canceling the Maui flight. "It's not quite Hawaii, but just having all of us together makes my day anywhere we are," Mary Jo wrote to her great-niece, Julia Lapp, in the summer of 2007.

That summer, Mary Jo and Robbie also flew to Arizona with Amy, her husband and their two children, Ali, 10, and Drew, 6. Then they saw the Grand Canyon and visited the desert resort town of Sedona. "I so love to spend time with them and make memories," Mary Jo wrote to Julia. "They are growing up way too fast."

All the while, Mary Jo was juggling cancer treatments and their varying effects. She avoided discussing her health in messages to Julia and others, except when responding to questions about how she was feeling. In mid-2007, Mary Jo answered an inquiry from Julia with encouraging news: "My scans show the tumors are shrinking so the meds are WORKING!!!!... I will remain on it indefinitely. Not crazy about that but thankful it is working." Soon after beginning the new regimen, Mary Jo reported she had inexplicably suffered a stress fracture in her foot. Cancer, and possibly her medications, had weakened her bones. But she joked as to how the injury may have happened: "I'm just WAY too athletic, I guess." Mary Jo considered the fracture only a minor inconvenience, telling Julia: "I feel good and that's what counts."

❧

No matter what else was going on in Mary Jo's life, she felt a renewed sense of purpose after making her crucial commitment to the Center. "I think the Center gave her momentum and a goal to attain," said her close friend, Martie Mehallis.

Yet Mary Jo downplayed her role in establishing the Center. A few months before it opened, Mary Jo wrote to Mary Fischer about her gift, saying that someone else surely would have stepped forward if she hadn't. "But I'm so glad it was ME," Mary Jo wrote. "I've gotten back more than I gave, I can tell you that."

Mary Jo also wrote that she wanted to tell the Center employees: "If it weren't for you all, this might not be."

John Prout, TriHealth president while the Cropper Center was coming together, said Mary Jo's timing was just right—and *she* was the right person.

"Mary Jo provided her story, her personality, her devotion to this cause," John said. "There is no question: It wouldn't have happened without her. We were able to bring along other donors because of her help."

The synergy between Susan and Mary Jo also was pivotal, John said: "They both had a commitment to the community, a commitment to the Center and the shared vision of serving women in a more compassionate, organized and supportive way." And, John said, Mary Jo had unknowingly tapped into the patient-comfort trend that was just emerging in healthcare at that time.

The "nuances" of an illness such as breast cancer make it more complex than many people realize, John said. "There are some aspects that are extremely important to the patient, but are not clinically related to your outcome," he said, such as whether a patient loses his or her hair and how surgeries, treatments and the disease itself can alter the patient's physical appearance. The new Cropper Center included programs to address such issues.

With all of that in mind, when the Center was being designed, hospital administrators gave the Center employees "more decision-making power than typically would be allowed," John said. "This was all about designing the caregiving experience, within a budget, within some parameters."

The Mary Jo Cropper Family Center for Breast Care opened in 2009 along with other outpatient imaging services. The Cropper Center later relocated to the new Thomas Comprehensive Care Center on the Bethesda North Hospital campus.

Years earlier, John had been forced to turn down Dr. Susan Weinberg when she approached him about a new Center. "I had to tell her that I believed in her vision, but we didn't have money in the budget," he said.

Nevertheless, Susan forged ahead and laid the groundwork for the future Cropper Center, John said.

"A program is not a building; it's a concept," he said. "The vision came first. We had the best program in the state and one of the best in the country, but we didn't have the facility to go along with it—or, the comfort, if you will."

It's hard to remember that, back when Susan first described her vision for the Center, her ideas were somewhat revolutionary, John said. "Back in those years, healthcare was a 'sport,' to use an analogy, of the 'star players,'" he said. There was little collaboration among professionals; everyone seemed to be wanting to make a name for himself or herself.

"And especially in breast cancer—much more than any other disease—you would get one answer from your radiologist, one answer from your oncologist and another answer from your gynecologist," he said. That was very confusing for patients, even though all of those specialists had the patient's best interests at heart. It was even stressful for the medical professionals, he said, because "culturally, I think people didn't know who was in charge."

So, when Susan Weinberg began the Breast Panel program, "to be able to come together and give a collaborative opinion, that was earth-shattering back then," John said. Since then, it has become standard practice. Throughout TriHealth, there are now panel discussions for various other types of disorders and diseases, emulating the process that was begun at the original Bethesda breast center. "Susan really is the mother of all that creation," said Jamie Easterling, who was the imaging administrator when the Cropper Center was being planned. "Susan was relentless with focusing on women's health. Because of her and the Center, I think the region jumped so far—with the help of Mary Jo, as well."

On a more personal note, Jamie also credits Susan for the part she played in his career. "Susan, back in the day, took a chance on me," he said. "And within a couple weeks, somebody retired; somebody quit. And I became the radiology manager for that campus." He said Susan was determined and tough. "I am who I am today because she drove certain perfections," said Jamie, who went on to become president of TriHealth's Good Samaritan Hospital. "As remarkable a physician as she is, she's almost a better person. And I've never seen anyone as passionate about getting things right as she is."

Under Susan's leadership, "there were a lot of 'firsts' in this region," even at the original breast center, Jamie said. To his knowledge, the Bethesda center was the first to employ "stereotactic biopsy," a process that uses radioactive seeds to help surgeons more precisely locate tumors.

Jamie also thinks the center became a leader in same-day results for diagnostic mammograms—the follow-up testing that is done after an initial screening mammogram reveals a possible abnormality. "Most often, you would get that diagnostic mammogram and go home and sit and worry about the results," Jamie said. Susan pushed for patients to get same-day results after those diagnostic tests, and even often after the screening tests, Jamie said.

Even though getting rapid results reduced patients' anxiety, some physicians bristled about changing the process. "Doctors didn't want patients to know the results before they, the doctors, had been told," Jamie said. "But Susan was such an advocate— she insisted that we need to do what is right for the patient. Still, you can imagine a doctor getting a phone call on a Friday afternoon from a frantic woman, saying, 'I've got breast cancer!' So, we had to work through some of that."

The period preceding the Center's creation was rocky in a lot of ways, John Prout said. American medicine as a whole was morphing "from a cottage industry to an organized system of care," John said. At the same time, Bethesda was undergoing a transformation. That was because of the corporate merger that created TriHealth, and also because of Bethesda's history. "People forget that Bethesda North was established as a satellite of the original Bethesda hospital on Oak Street in Cincinnati," John said, "so it was never designed for patient care, like most hospitals."

The Cropper Center was important to the hospital itself because it was one of the first tangible signs that "people were paying attention to Bethesda … you're not a satellite anymore," John said. The Center was also a physical representation of a shift in philosophy, he said: "This is not a business project. It's about improving care for patients—and outpatient care was the future of medicine."

Pointing out that the Cropper Center pioneered the Cincinnati region's first nurse-navigator program for breast care, John said, "We were a leader in Ohio, the Midwest, and maybe beyond. From the bottom of my heart, I can say that this program has added to the body of knowledge for patient care."

The Center became a model for other healthcare programs of all types, John said, not solely for breast cancer. Now, throughout healthcare, the goal is to put together "a plan of care," rather than just asking, "What's the next step?" he said.

Because of initiatives that the Cropper Center would be taking, its Grand Opening felt different than many others John had witnessed during his decades-long history in healthcare. "There was more excitement about how this is going to help," he said, "as opposed to, 'This is the end of the project.'"

In the world of medicine, one of the surest signs of excellence is accreditation. That's why certain certificates on the Center's walls are especially meaningful.

One is from the National Accreditation Program for Breast Centers. The Cropper Center was the first in Greater Cincinnati to attain this accreditation, and the sixth one in Ohio, a Bethesda news release said. That quality-assurance program, administered through the American College of Surgeons, requires extensive proof that the facility meets detailed standards in five areas:

· A "team approach" to coordinate care and treatment plans
  among specialists
· Education and support programs available to patients
· Tracking data that are considered "quality indicators" in
  breast cancer diagnosis and treatment
· Keeping track of patients' health status and care
· Information about clinical trials and new treatments

Tina German, a nurse who started working at the precursor to the Cropper Center, said the staff was proud to see the Center lead the way with that accreditation in 2010. Ten years later, four other breast centers in the region made the list, alongside twenty other Ohio facilities, including large, well-known places such as the Cleveland Clinic. But Tina said, "I think we can match exactly what all of these big centers do. I go to conferences and I hear, 'This is up-and-coming,' and I say to myself,

'Well, we do that already.' We have had some visionaries who put their hearts and souls into this and made the Center what it is today."

Another important certification at the Center, which Tina and several other staffers hold, is Certified Navigator-Breast Nurse. Tina earned that distinction in 2011, three years after the National Consortium of Breast Centers Inc. established it. The certification is intended to set standards of achievement for nurse navigators and to "enhance patient safety, quality of care and delivery of services," the organization's website says. Another goal is to recognize professionals for attaining a wealth of knowledge in this specialized field.

Mary Jo believed it was important for a newly diagnosed cancer patient to have a qualified professional, such as Tina, "to hold the patient's hand," both literally and figuratively. Mary Jo, in only a few interactions with Tina, emphasized how much she valued the role that a nurse navigator would fulfill. Mary Jo also wrote about that in a note to a friend: "I have 'been there,' and I know how frightening and confusing those first days are when newly diagnosed. To have compassionate, caring people 'walk' you though it, it is a Godsend."

Summed up in a single sentence, Tina said this is what the nurse-navigator role entails: "I guide a newly diagnosed cancer patient on the journey to survivorship."

Even years later, Tina said she and other nurse navigators considered Mary Jo to be a driving force for them, "a silent partner" in their daily work.

Tina pointed out that the Center's practice isn't limited to cancer. In fact, the Center mostly handles thousands of routine mammograms that are negative for any life-threatening findings. Some Center patients are diagnosed with benign breast conditions or come for treatment of breast injuries. "That is why it is called 'the Cropper Center for Breast *Care*,'" Tina said, "not the 'cancer' center."

If a mammogram reveals an area of concern, the patient is asked to return for a diagnostic mammogram. The next step, if warranted, is a biopsy. And, if that reveals cancer is present, Tina makes a difficult telephone call to the patient. It usually goes something like this:

"Hi, I'm Tina. I've been a nurse working with breast patients for more than twenty years, and I need to inform you that the test was positive."

Often, the patient will start crying. Some people go silent. Others ask a lot of questions, starting with, "Am I gonna die?"

And Tina will respond: "I'm here for you. I know you have a lot of questions, but here is the next step…. A lot of times, 'I'll say this is not a death sentence.'… It's much more survivable today than it was in the past. You could go to the mall today and just ask how many women have had breast cancer—and a lot of them all around you would raise their hand."

Tina reassures terrified patients: "I'm gonna get you through this. You're going to feel like you're crossing the Grand Canyon without a bridge, but we'll put the planks in place for you. And, a year from now, you're going to be on the other side, waving at me and saying, 'It was nice knowing you; I'll see you next year.'"

Sometimes, the outcome is sad and tragic. But often, patients who once felt hopeless will live a long time after their diagnoses—and they still stay in touch with Tina. "Years later, I have patients telling me, 'If it weren't for you, I would've never made it.' And they'll be hugging and kissing on me," Tina said.

Tina is thankful for those experiences. "I think the angels put me in this job," she said. "I haven't had breast cancer, but I've had other major health conditions, and I've been doing this for over twenty years, so I do understand."

Educating patients is an important aspect of Tina's job. Patients once shied away from information. But, with support from the Bethesda Foundation and the American Cancer Society, the Center stocks a resource library filled with books. Holding up one of those, *Breast Cancer Clear and Simple,* Tina says, "it laid in a drawer for a while; the patients didn't look at it." That has changed. Now people are willing to read that book and others, Tina said, because societal attitudes have changed. She thinks social media has played a big role in that shift. People openly post details of their cancer diagnoses and treatments on Facebook and

Instagram. "So just having other people out there, sharing their stories, that makes people more receptive to getting information about it," Tina said. "Now they *want* that education; you're not forcing them to learn something."

Billie Burrus, who was hired as a mammography technologist when Bethesda's original breast center was founded in late 1995, assumed a new role after the Cropper Center opened. As Imaging Navigator, Billie schedules patients for a complex series of procedures and follow-ups—a process that often spans several years. Billie connects each newly diagnosed patient to Tina or another nurse navigator.

Billie also plays an important unofficial role: "the mother of everybody" at the Center. Billie serves as a mentor for young women in the Center's training program for mammography technologists, which is certified through the American College of Radiology. And she takes on a motherly tone in her work with patients. Decades of experience in the breast health field have made her acutely aware that, out of all the types of imaging that can be done on a person, breast imaging tends to be fraught with the most emotion.

"Your breasts are part of your personality, your 'womanliness,'" Billie said. "Women's breasts have always been on display, as part of who you are … and that's why some women today still don't want to verbalize that they've had breast cancer."

Decades ago, in the 1920s and '30s, many women were so ashamed of having breast cancer that "they would have a mastectomy and they would never share that with their own children," Billie said. "They would have hidden it by wearing baggy clothes." That was a sad situation for the woman and for her descendants, who would be unaware of the family's history of breast cancer. And that might prevent future generations from getting the early screenings they would need. Now, however, most women do inform close relatives about their cancer, Billie said.

Still, the intense emotions haven't changed. Even just being told that a biopsy is needed to check an abnormality can be enough to make some patients "feel like some of their womanhood is gone," Billie said. She views it as part of her job to address those heavy-duty feelings. "It takes a certain personality to deal with patients' emotions, anxieties and fears, and also to help their families," she said. "It's not for everybody, but I feel very blessed to do it."

Billie said she felt especially fortunate to be working in the Cropper Center, because of the atmosphere, the staff's caring attitude and the level of expertise there.

"First-timers or even return patients say, 'It's such a lovely facility. We feel comfortable here. We feel taken care of here,'" Billie said. "We let our patients know: You're doing all the things that you should do; you're in the best place that you can possibly be, where you're going to get the best, most comprehensive care possible."

Billie's colleague, Tina, the nurse navigator, put it this way: "A mammogram isn't the most fun thing in the world to go through. But for women who come here to get one, it's impressive when you walk in the front door. It's a pretty place. It's exquisite. And the artwork, well that really just blows people away."

Local artists donated original paintings to be hung in the building—and then would be sold on demand or auctioned to earn money for the Center. Jamie Easterling, the imaging administrator, said his mother-in-law, Jean Vance, was a driving force behind that initiative. At the time, Jean ran the art program at Miami University in nearby Oxford, Ohio. "She said to me, 'Jamie, you *have* to put art in that building—*real* art," he said. "She showed me how art can create a healing atmosphere at some other facilities."

The idea gained traction. Two hundred artists applied to have their work showcased at the Center, Jamie said.

As the Center neared completion, Jean told the building's architects, "Don't worry about the colors. I'll just make it work," Jamie recalled. She also said, "Art just 'happens.' You can't place things; it has to just 'live.'"

In late July 2009, the weekend before the building was to open, volunteers stepped up to hang 115 pieces of artwork.

"They opened three or four bottles of wine and they just started hanging art. And then the building opened—and no one had ever seen this artwork, so it became an art gallery," Jamie said. "We saw women coming to the Center together, to not only look at art in the building, but to start making a day of it when they would come to get their mammograms, and then go to lunch."

Visitors could buy the artwork "right off the wall," Jamie said, with prices ranging from $20 to $20,000. Then, "every year, they would take the art down, have an auction, and bring new pieces in," Jamie said. The proceeds went to the Bethesda Foundation in support of the Center.

At the first art auction, Dr. Susan Weinberg spotted a painting she wanted to purchase. Susan was drawn to it partly because it was entitled, *Friends,* which made her think of Mary Jo. Susan intended to buy the painting and donate it back to the Center in honor of her friend.

But Susan and Mary Jo kept out-bidding each other on that same painting, sending the price higher and higher. Finally, Susan prevailed. "I won the bid and dedicated it to her that evening," Susan said. The painting depicts women relaxing on a bench, enjoying ice cream together, with a collection of shopping bags sitting at their feet.

Ever since, that special piece of artwork has remained a fixture in the Center, a place that Jamie Easterling called "a masterpiece"—one created by two friends named Susan and Mary Jo, plus a bunch of other people who cared.

9

Declining and Soaring

Mary Jo was in high spirits after the Center's big launch, but her body was growing weaker than most people ever would have guessed.

And few people were aware of the other stresses Mary Jo had faced. While dealing with her own cancer, she also anguished over the breast cancer diagnosis of her oldest sister, Sandy Perry. Her cancer surfaced while the Center was still in the planning stages. On top of that, Mary Jo's other sister, Gail Norris, was diagnosed a few months after the Center opened.

Mary Jo stepped partly into the navigator role for both of her sisters, guiding them to the care they needed. When Sandy was diagnosed with cancer in late 2007, Mary Jo broke that news to Sandy's daughter, Cathy Chasteen. "Auntie Mary called me and said, 'Your mom has breast cancer,'" Cathy said. That pronouncement left Cathy stunned, saddened and worried.

But, as usual, Mary Jo took a reassuring tone. She convinced Cathy that everything would be all right because Sandy's cancer had been caught very early. Mary Jo said she was betting that Sandy's cancer probably wouldn't come back, based on the stage and other circumstances. Dr. Ching Ho, who later became co-director of the Cropper Center, performed Sandy's lumpectomy. Mary Jo was there for her surgery, Sandy said. And Sandy, who was 72 at the time of her diagnosis, remained cancer-free more than a dozen years later. She never underwent chemotherapy; she just had surgery and radiation. The relationship between Sandy and her daughter, Cathy, strengthened because of Sandy's cancer. "It helped bring us closer together," Cathy said, "because I realized she might not be around."

Mary Jo and her immediate family enjoyed a final trip to Hawaii in 2010. Front row: grandchildren Sophie and Lily Cropper, Ali Settlemyre, Drew Settlemyre and Josie Cropper. Back row: Spence and Dana Cropper, Amy Settlemyre, Mary Jo and her husband, Robbie.

In early 2010, Gail, the middle Stolle sister, became a breast cancer patient at the Center. Gail was in disbelief when she found herself in that position just a few months after attending the Center's 2009 Grand Opening. Gail remembers being so proud of Mary Jo that day—and afterward, Gail was so thankful for the Center's services. Although Gail always believed that she needed to take care of her "baby sister," Mary Jo, when Gail was diagnosed with cancer, the two "reversed roles," said Gail's daughter, Sylvia Norris. "Auntie Mary took such good care of Mom and let her know what was ahead of her, as Mom did not like the unknown. Auntie Mary was there while Mom was waiting for the Breast Center to call with her test results." Like Sandy, Gail was fortunate that her cancer was found quickly, and no chemotherapy was required. She has gone more than a decade with no sign of recurrence.

Mary Jo's son, Spence, said, "Mom wanted to help both of them as much as she could," despite the limitations that her own illness imposed.

As Mary Jo's disease continued its onslaught, she mostly kept her discomfort to herself. She didn't want other people to worry about her. Nor did she want their pity. She spent her energy wisely, getting the most out of whatever time she had left—but not necessarily for herself. Some people might turn inward and succumb to selfish desires. But not Mary Jo. She soldiered on, helping others even as her strength waned.

Some days, just picking up the phone or putting pen to paper felt like a powerlifting workout. But she did those things anyway. She believed it was important to help as many people as she could. And she discovered that setting aside her own worries was therapeutic.

Mary Jo's friends marveled at her selflessness. Her college roommate, Martie Mehallis, was visiting from Florida in 2010 when something caught her eye in Mary Jo's home office. On one wall, "there were about twenty names on a little piece of paper," Martie recalled.

She joked with Mary Jo: "Oh, I see you have some new friends. I guess you're replacing me."

"No, those are people I need to call today," Mary Jo said. "Most of them have breast cancer and I need to check on them."

Incredulous, Martie asked: "You're going to call *all* those people *today*?" And then, Martie recalls, "She said, 'Yes, of course!' As if, 'Why would you question that?' I thought it was a week-long to-do list. Not so. That was for *that day*."

Because Mary Jo had such a long history with breast cancer, she thought it was valuable to share her knowledge with people who were newcomers to the disease, Martie said: "She was like a pioneer who knew the pitfalls that they were going to face, and she thought maybe she could make it easier on them."

But Mary Jo's kind gestures weren't reserved solely for people with cancer. "Even if you didn't do something for her—even if she just heard you did something for someone—you would get a note," Martie said. "What made her that way? Cancer. I think she was more aware of other people suffering, and she wanted to encourage anyone who tried to help other people in any way."

Talitha Colston, one of the Wahines who regularly hung out with Mary Jo, expressed the group's consensus: "We would always say that we wish we could be as strong as Mary Jo."

"Every time we found out someone had cancer, we'd let Mary Jo know," Talitha said. "And she just did her own thing. She would email, write a note of encouragement, or if she felt good enough, maybe visit that person—or just do something really nice, anonymously."

A very ill woman named Cindy didn't have a comfortable chair, so Mary Jo bought her an expensive black leather recliner—an act of kindness that Mary Jo's friends discovered in a round-about way, not from her. "And that's just the one recliner that we know about," Mary Jo's sister-in-law, Ginny Kuntz, said. "There could have been ten others."

There's more to the story about Cindy. She had always wanted to go on a hot-air balloon ride—and Mary Jo made that wish come true, too. Later, Ginny ran into the balloonist who described Cindy and her mother enjoying a glorious trip aloft. The two women sang gospel hymns as they drifted beneath the clouds.

"Those were the kinds of special things that Mary Jo did for anybody and everybody," Ginny said. "Not many people are like that."

All the while, Mary Jo forced herself to stay active with her family. That was one way she demonstrated her love for them. But one trip exposed how badly her health had declined.

The entire family had flown to California in late 2009, in time to watch the Ohio State Buckeyes play the Oregon Ducks in the 2010 Rose Bowl. Throughout the five-day trip, Mary Jo hardly left her hotel room. But come game time on New Year's Day 2010, "she was a trouper," Spence said. "She never complained once even though it was a long day for her." For Mary Jo, the payoff was worth the effort. She got to spend time with her family and was able to see OSU win, 26–17.

From that time forward, Mary Jo started taking steps that telegraphed: Her light was dimming. And she knew it.

Although the Center was a major legacy, Mary Jo also did a lot of little things to leave lasting effects on people she loved.

Within weeks of the Rose Bowl trip, Mary Jo lovingly compiled a cookbook entitled, "Cropper/Stolle Family Recipes." Using a custom font that mimicked her distinct backward-slant handwriting, Mary Jo typed about three dozen family favorites, including her mom's sour cream coffeecake and her dad's German potato salad. Mary Jo had the pages laminated and bound. Inside, there's also a "recipe" for comic relief, so to speak. A smattering of typographical errors produced gems such as this one: Instead of "Crabmeat Pizza," there was "*Crapmeat* Pizza." Maybe those typos could be blamed on "chemo-brain," an effect on cancer patients' sharpness. Or maybe Mary Jo made them intentionally, hoping to evoke some smiles and laughs, even in tough times.

Around the time Mary Jo produced the cookbook, she also used her signature font to type love letters to all five grandchildren. Each one was carefully crafted, lending credence to the theory that the cookbook typos may have been committed on purpose. Among the sweet messages to her "grands" was this one, written to Dana and Spence's youngest daughter:

Dear Miss Lily,

We get such a kick out of you, Lily. You have different things that you will say that are so cute, and we have come to call them "Lilyisms."… Once, when I was wearing my wigs because of chemo, I told you I wished I had your hair. You ever so quickly told me it was attached, and I could not have it!! Another time, on an airplane, you announced very loudly, "Mimi, do you have your wig on?" I loved that everyone on the plane knew I did not have hair.…

I have written all these little notes to all the grandchildren for you to read when you are a little older and just might forget what Mimi was like. Well, most importantly, I want you to remember how much I loved each and every one of you.…

My favorite times with all of you were when we went on family trips. I tried to plan a lot of them so you all would have memories too.…

Please know how much I love you and will ALWAYS love you. Even from Heaven above, I will be watching down on all of you.…

Much love forever, Lily.
MIMI

Another sentimental step Mary Jo took in early 2010: She tried to re-establish some semblance of the annual Stolle family reunions. A few years after her dad, Ralph Stolle, died, the annual gatherings fell by the wayside. Other relatives had learned that pulling off the event took more effort than they realized.

Longing to rekindle that tradition, Mary Jo organized a family get-together at her house on March 20, 2010. It made her happy to bring together relatives who had drifted apart. About sixty people shared ham at that pre-Easter gathering, along with cupcakes, wine and memories. It was the first large Stolle gathering in about a decade.

Mary Jo later wrote to her niece, Cathy Chasteen: "I am so glad we could have the reunion…. That day gave me such peace. I know everyone enjoyed themselves … you could just tell."

Mary Jo also wrote: "Now, my goal is for you all to do this at least once a year!!!!!"

The way that sentence was written, Mary Jo was clearly implying that she was passing the torch to someone else. The next time, she probably wouldn't feel well enough to participate—or she might no longer be around at all.

No one wanted to admit it, but Mary Jo was composing her swan song—and the reunion, the love letters and the cookbook were among the final flourishes.

Meanwhile, Mary Jo's loved ones were reciprocating. They started taking steps, big and small, to express their love and appreciation for her—while there was still time to do that.

Mary Jo's niece, Sylvia Norris, admired the example her Auntie Mary set. "She taught people not to be selfish, to help others and to love the people you're with," Sylvia said. "She made me think about being a better person."

As Mary Jo's condition worsened, Sylvia thought of a novel way to honor her aunt.

Mary Jo had grown up around horses, and had a special memory associated with Secretariat, winner of the 1973 Triple Crown. Mary Jo and Robbie had watched Secretariat win the Kentucky Derby that year—and they celebrated with champagne toasts and a rose from the winning horse's famed Garland of Roses. After that, Mary Jo kept a picture of Secretariat on display to remind her of that noteworthy occasion.

Also, Mary Jo had always encouraged Sylvia's interest in horse-breeding and horse-racing. So, at the mini family reunion in March 2010, Sylvia revealed that she had decided to name a horse in honor of Mary Jo. Sylvia came up with the name, "Mary J Chardonnay," a blend of her aunt's name plus her favorite variety of wine. "Auntie Mary loved the name," Sylvia said. "She laughed and said it was a perfect name." So, Sylvia did, in fact, give that name to a bay Standardbred that had just been born that spring on her farm in Clearcreek Township, Warren County. Unfortunately, the horse never got to meet its namesake; the horse was later sold to another farm. Still, just looking at her other horses still reminds Sylvia of Mary Jo, who would often talk about riding horses on SanMarGale farm.

On May 19, 2010, a gesture from one of Mary Jo's granddaughters touched the hearts of everyone who learned about it. On a piece of notebook paper, Spence and Dana's daughter, Josie, wrote a letter to her grandma, thanking her for a $250 reward for making good grades. Mary Jo had always taught her grandchildren to give a small portion of their money to charitable causes. But Josie, then age 9, had other plans. She wrote, in part:

> *Dear Mimi:*
>
> *Thank you for the money. You said I only had to donate $50 of it, but I decided to give ALL $250 to the Breast Care Center in your honor....*
>
> *I love you and you mean a lot to me, and I know that the Breast Care Center means a lot to you....*
>
> *Another reason I choose the Breast Care Center is because I know how hard people work to help others fight breast cancer. It also costs lots of money for equipment. Thanks again. Love you!*
>
> *Love,*
> *Josie*

Hardly anyone knew it, but in early 2010, Mary Jo wrote a little letter that landed with a mighty thump.

Brenda Bingham, the Lebanon Presbyterian Church secretary, had just returned from vacationing with her husband. They had been to Hawaii, a spot that Brenda knew Mary Jo loved.

"I got the mail, and there was a letter for me. I thought it might be an invitation to a party or something," Brenda said. "But I opened it, and within five seconds, I was praying and in tears." It was a letter from Mary Jo. It began by acknowledging that Mary Jo knew Brenda was on vacation. But the next part set off Brenda's emotional reaction: *When you get back, please let me know when we can meet. I need to start making plans for my funeral.*

"I was praying that God was healing her and I was crying for her family," Brenda said. "I didn't want it to be the end. I just didn't want it to be real."

Brenda was too upset to tell her husband what the letter said. That was because Mary Jo had meant so much to her personally—and to so many other people in the church. Mary Jo and the rest of the Stolle-Cropper family were deeply interwoven in the fabric of the church community.

Time and time again, Brenda and the church's pastor, the Rev. Peter Larson, had seen Mary Jo in action, helping others. "Charity can be very impersonal, just writing checks," Peter said. But Mary Jo made it personal. "She was the fairy godmother who would find out a need or a wish—and just make it happen," Peter said.

Both he and Brenda were aware of the story about the woman named Cindy receiving a recliner from Mary Jo. Cindy, who was a member of the church, eventually died from ovarian cancer. Mary Jo's thoughtful actions for Cindy showed that Mary Jo had truly followed in her dad's philanthropic footsteps. Father and daughter both gave freely.

That quality—and so many others—made Brenda admire Mary Jo. "She was always inspiring me to be the best person I could be," Brenda said. "We give lip service to so many things, maybe give someone a pat on the back. But Mary Jo believed that wasn't enough. She believed: You *do* something. She walked the walk and talked the talk. She never said anything she did not believe. And she cared for everybody."

As much as Brenda was distressed over the notion of planning a funeral for Mary Jo, she was also honored that Mary Jo wanted her help. When Mary Jo showed up for the meeting, she and Brenda sat down in a prayer room—one that Mary Jo and her sister-in-law, Ginny Kuntz, had established about three years earlier. "It had always been a goal of ours to have an actual prayer room where people can go in and pray and be with God," Brenda said. Mary Jo and Ginny stepped up. They furnished and decorated that room together. Ever since, the room has been a favorite spot for parishioners seeking solitude.

Mary Jo and Brenda got some tears out of the way, then tried to get down to business. Organizing funeral services was part of Brenda's job. But during three decades as church secretary, she had rarely seen a parishioner plan his or her own funeral. It was another example of Mary Jo's desire to make other people comfortable. "She didn't want to put this burden on anyone else; she didn't want her family to have to make any decisions," Brenda said. "And she wanted to accommodate everyone who would show up."

"We were just there, sitting on the bench and having an open and honest conversation," Brenda said. "She seemed happy when I told her that I would be more than willing to help her with anything that she needed. I could see a little wave of relief come over her." Mary Jo pulled out a piece of paper. She had written down many thoughts about the funeral and reception. Then, together, the two women brainstormed. Brenda filled three pages of notes. As the meeting wound down, Brenda and Mary Jo prayed. And cried. "Maybe she was crying because I was crying," Brenda said. "But I was praying that God would find a miracle."

Among all the people who knew Mary Jo well, Martie Mehallis probably has tucked away the largest trove of secrets about her. As Mary Jo's college roommate, fellow breast cancer survivor and decades-long confidante, Martie stood shoulder-to-shoulder with Mary Jo through the highs, the lows and everything in between.

And Martie knew, better than most people, that Mary Jo had likely opened the final chapter of her life in early 2010. "Mary Jo's cancer was a different kind than I had and much more serious," Martie said.

While Mary Jo was solidifying plans for the mini reunion that March, she had admitted to several relatives that "there had been some major changes" with her health. That was an understatement. Mary Jo's longtime oncologist, Dr. Robert Cody, had put her on some new medications that month. He was aiming to extend her life. But the side effects were awful. In an email dated April 1, 2010, Mary Jo was frank with Martie: "I went to Dr. Cody and told him how very sick I'd been. I was ready to call it quits. But he tells me that I've responded quite well to the new chemo after only two doses and have expanded my life from weeks to months."

Mary Jo loved Dr. Cody, even though he was "not warm and fuzzy," Martie said. Dr. Cody tended to cut to the chase, she said, but Mary Jo was convinced he genuinely cared about her. "He was very supportive of her decisions," Martie said.

Despite the progress Mary Jo showed that spring, she was running out of steam. As a last resort, Martie persuaded Mary Jo to visit another doctor at The Ohio State University; Martie's husband, Steve, arranged it. "The doctor there commented that she didn't outwardly appear as sick as she really was," Martie said. Mary Jo was that good at downplaying effects of her illness. But the OSU doctor agreed with Dr. Cody: There was nothing left for Mary Jo to try.

On May 12, 2010, Martie received an email from Mary Jo that made her heart sink: "Went to Dr. Cody to tell him I'm done with chemo. I've been on this poison nonsense for eight years.... Today was tough."

Martie couldn't blame her friend. "You just reach a point where your bad days outnumber your good days, and you ask yourself, 'Why am I bothering with all of this?'" Martie said. "She fought that demon for almost twenty years; she was exhausted."

Every sword, every shield had failed to vanquish Mary Jo's foe; it was time to lay down arms. Mary Jo expected the beast to rise up and quickly overpower her. Instead, when the dust settled, she was still standing—at least for a little while longer.

To Mary Jo's surprise, she rallied. After the chemicals cleared out of her body, Mary Jo felt as if she had stepped out of a dark, dank cave and into the bright, warm sunlight.

"She was feeling good and doing well," her sister, Sandy Perry, said. Then she lowered her eyes and said, "But it didn't last."

One by one, Mary Jo's loved ones were forced to accept the truth: Mary Jo's time was growing short.

Mary Jo's sister-in-law, Ginny Kuntz, remembers that was on her mind during a Norris Lake outing sometime in 2010. Ginny, Mary Jo and others were going on a boat ride. Wearing both a wig and a hat, Mary Jo kept saying she felt uncomfortably hot. "And we kept telling her, 'Take it off. It's okay. You're among friends,'" Ginny said. Mary Jo, who liked to look well-groomed and "pulled together," was reluctant. Finally, she relented. "There she was, our bald captain," Ginny said. It hurt Ginny's heart to see Mary Jo that way. But she and the other boat passengers didn't want to see Mary Jo suffer. She had already done enough of that.

Under the hot sun, the image was seared into Ginny's memory: Hatless and hairless, Mary Jo was steering the boat across the glistening lake while the breeze blew everyone else's hair. That unforgettable picture embodied powerful truths about that moment in time. The ravages of cancer had stolen Mary Jo's hair, but not her dignity. Her "crew" loved and accepted her, just as she was. And Mary Jo smiled, savoring the freedom of guiding the boat wherever she pleased, unashamed of how she looked and reveling in how she felt. For the first time in a long time, she felt a little more in control—and almost like herself again.

Reinvigorated, Mary Jo began planning a vacation that would become the crown jewel of her "making memories" collection. Ginny put together most of the itinerary.

The eight-day trip to Hawaii began June 24, 2010—the final trip that travel agent Marsha Falknor would book for Mary Jo. By now, Mary Jo's fear of flying had diminished. After facing cancer, nothing could make her afraid anymore.

Mary Jo's daughter, Amy, said the trip was the most memorable one the family had ever experienced. "It was just so nice to see Mom feeling really good after she got the chemo out of her system," Amy said.

Mary Jo and Robbie Cropper were delighted to share a slice of paradise with both of their children, all five grandchildren, Ginny and Ron Kuntz and other relatives. First, the family stayed three days on "The Garden Island," Kauai. Then they rented a private home for five days in Kapalua, on Maui island, nestled amid swaths of contrasting colors. The whiteness of the sand beaches. The blueness of the Pacific's waters. The brightness of the sky. The greenness of the plants and trees dotted with a rainbow of fruits and flowers. The blackness of the volcanic mountains.

This, more than any prescription from the doctor, soothed Mary Jo's body. And being there with her family nourished her soul. "We had a wonderful time and I felt great," Mary Jo later said in an email to a friend. Mary Jo couldn't believe how awful she had felt earlier that year, and how much better she felt now, without chemo in her system.

As a surprise, Ginny arranged for a minister to come and perform a Hawaiian chant and prayer over Mary Jo. The entire group went with Mary Jo, who rode in a golf cart, to a little crescent beach for the ceremony. "I think she was touched because she didn't know it was coming," Ginny said.

Years later, Ginny could still picture Mary Jo smiling as she watched her grandkids splashing in the giant swimming pool at the rented house in Hawaii. Maybe Mary Jo had even flashed back to her own carefree days as a child, swimming with her sisters and friends in the pool at SanMarGale.

At poolside in Hawaii, Ginny saw tears trickling down Mary Jo's cheeks—one of the few times that happened. "I hardly ever saw Mary cry," Ginny said. "I would see her shed tears, but not really cry. She was brave through all of this." Ginny thinks that

Mary Jo was wistful about watching her grandchildren playing. "She probably knew this might be the last time she would get to see that," Ginny said.

The high point of the trip, without question, was the night when the family splurged and hired a chef to prepare a private meal at their rented home. "We sat outside and just had this beautiful dinner," Amy said. "Everything was so wonderful and fresh—like mahi-mahi that was just caught that day."

There was no corralling the kids into vehicles and traveling to a restaurant, no shopping for ingredients, no cooking, no bothering with post-meal cleanup. Just food, togetherness and happiness in the loveliest of settings.

"It was so nice just to sit there with our family at this gorgeous home and to have this special dinner, looking at the ocean and the palm trees—just the most spectacular view all around," Amy said. "And seeing Mom feeling good just made it so much more enjoyable for everyone, in every way. It made her forget a little bit that she had cancer."

When the trip was being planned, Mary Jo's family had been concerned that she might not feel well enough to enjoy the experience. "But she was just determined to make this very special for the kids and for all of us," Amy said. "And it was like God just allowed it to happen."

Mary Jo's rejuvenation wasn't quite the cure-all miracle that church secretary Brenda Bingham had beseeched the Lord to provide. But Mary Jo's improved health was still a tremendous blessing to her and her family, even if it was temporary.

In Hawaii, the word, "aloha," is not solely a greeting or a farewell. That word also is used to express feelings of love, peace and compassion. And this visit to Hawaii, more than any other Cropper family vacation, overflowed with the aloha spirit. Yet it was tinged with sadness. "I think everyone knew it was our last trip with her," Amy said, "and it was hard because we knew that." Almost a decade later, Amy looked back on her mother's final Hawaiian excursion and said, "I'm so glad we did it, because we did make such happy memories."

As summer turned to autumn, Mary Jo knew that discontinuing chemo had been the right decision. Her body needed a break. Powerful anti-cancer drugs had battered her healthy cells almost as much as they had attacked her cancerous ones. Still, Mary Jo faced a dilemma: Should she jump into the ring for one more round?

On November 1, 2010, she emailed her dear friend Martie Mehallis, saying that her oncologist, Dr. Robert Cody, had found indicators that her health was better without the chemotherapy. "He told me he frankly feels if I had continued on chemo, we would not be having a conversation now," Mary Jo wrote. No new clinical trials had surfaced for Mary Jo to try. But she had the option of going back on chemotherapy drugs again—which didn't appeal to her. "Why would I want to go through that again when there are NO assurances it will work?" she asked.

Mary Jo had already decided the answer to that question. It no longer made sense to pump her body full of chemicals. Now, after five months on the upswing, Mary Jo could feel her strength ebbing. The end of the road was relentlessly creeping toward her.

Martie replied: "Good friends don't let each other suffer alone, and you NEVER complain, so I know you're suffering." She volunteered to come be with Mary Jo anytime.

As usual, Mary Jo pushed herself to continue with activities, despite discomfort. Large amounts of fluid would accumulate in her abdomen, a byproduct of everything her body had weathered. At times, doctors drained as much as three liters of fluid, Mary Jo told Martie. On November 12, a day after one of those awful procedures, Mary Jo emailed Martie and said she would need to have the fluid drained *weekly*. Then, without skipping a beat, Mary Jo said, "Have a lot of running to do, so better get in my shower and step it up. Tonight is our big gala for Kindervelt." That would be the final time Mary Jo would attend a fundraiser for Kindervelt, a group that supports Cincinnati Children's Hospital Medical Center. Eventually, Mary Jo decided to discontinue the drainage procedures—and to stop all therapeutic measures.

Even during tough times like these, Mary Jo never lost her sense of humor. Her son, Spence, chuckles when recounting an incident that happened during one of his mom's many medical appointments in late 2010. She and Spence had reported to the registration desk at the Center. When the receptionist asked her name, Mary Jo responded, "Mary Jo Cropper." Then the receptionist said, "And can you spell that last name for me?" Spence and his mom didn't have the heart to tell the receptionist what they were thinking: "Just look on the outside of the building, above the door, and you'll see how it's spelled."

Instead of being indignant that her name wasn't immediately recognized, Mary Jo got a kick out of it. She started cracking up. So did Spence. "And the poor lady who asked, 'How do you spell it?' had no idea why this lady is laughing," Spence said. Neither Mary Jo nor Spence felt slighted by the receptionist's failure to recognize Mary Jo's name. In fact, they thought it was entirely understandable, given that the receptionist was dealing with patients for the entire imaging center building, not just for the Mary Jo Cropper Family Center for Breast Care. Later, Spence was glad that his mom was able to enjoy a moment of levity. "It was what she needed that day," he said. "God brought her a little comic relief."

When Thanksgiving rolled around, Mary Jo was grateful that she would have no hostess responsibilities. She and Robbie had been invited to join at least a half-dozen other relatives at Spence and Dana's home. Mary Jo emailed her great-niece, Julia Lapp, and said she especially enjoyed dishes prepared by Dana's mom, Rosie VanDeGrift. "Even though we all brought something, Rosie's food always outshines everyone's," Mary Jo wrote. "She's a marvelous cook."

In response to Julia's question about how she was feeling, Mary Jo responded, "I'm feeling so-so.... I never know how I'll feel from one day to the next." It was unusual for Mary Jo to even admit that much. So she must have been feeling truly awful. Still, she wrote, "I'm just grateful to be here. I love this time of year and love the excitement of all the kids." Except for the oldest grandchild, Amy's daughter, Ali, her grandkids still "sort of" believed in Santa Claus, Mary Jo reported.

The family had hired the same man to pose as Santa for several years—and were planning to do so again, Mary Jo said. She didn't mention that Ali's belief in Santa disintegrated the year she looked outside and saw something that didn't fit the Santa mythology. Amy remembers Ali asking: "Why is Santa arriving in a van?"

Mary Jo wrote to Julia that her other grandchildren sometimes "seem skeptical" as to whether Santa was real. They all would climb onto his lap anyhow and talk about the magic of Christmas. And seeing that made Mary Jo happy.

Mary Jo seized this moment to tell Julia that she and her husband were fantastic parents. And she congratulated the couple for having another child on the way. "God knows how great you are with your kids and he's just rewarding you with more because they will certainly grow up to be as good a person as you both are," Mary Jo wrote. "You have such patience and so enjoy your children. It's wonderful to watch."

That message, which was sent on November 29, 2010, was the last one Julia received from her great-aunt. It was signed, "Love, Auntie M."

Then came Mary Jo's usual Christmas cards—the final batch, depicting a trio of Scottie dogs with plaid bows tied around their necks.

In December, Mary Jo enjoyed one last outing with her two good friends from the Bethesda North campus, Dr. Susan Weinberg and Bethesda Foundation representative Mary Fischer. Of course, Mary Jo sent a thank-you note, telling Mary: "It was *so* nice being able to enjoy a glass of wine with you, and have some personal time with Sue. It was a very special evening for me."

At Christmastime, the last pictures of Mary Jo were taken. Spence has a hard time looking at them. Even though Mary Jo is wearing tastefully applied makeup and a beautiful red blouse with a black silky scarf, her eyes had lost their luster. The photographer who took the pictures, Mary Jo's niece, Kris Marr, did a lovely job, "with the best of intentions," Spence said. But the camera doesn't lie; Mary Jo just didn't look like she felt well. "The life was already sucked out of her at that point," Spence said. "She was a shell of who she was."

Mary Jo was also not quite herself at a holiday get-together of Stolle relatives at The Golden Lamb, an historic Lebanon restaurant. She did her best to participate in the festivities. But Spence sensed something different about his mother. "She had that look in her eyes—for her, it was a goodbye," Spence said. "I don't want to say she gave up, but she was drained. The look told me, 'I'm tired of going through all of this.'"

Spence had taken her to the gathering. Before long, his mom said, "I'm not feeling well. Will you take me home?"

During the drive back to her house, mother and son had an honest end-of-life discussion. As hard as it was, Spence appreciated that talk. "It made her passing so much easier," he said. "I mourned *with her*, while she was still here."

One of Mary Jo's biggest concerns was how her husband, Robbie, would fare without her companionship after more than forty-four years of marriage. She asked Spence to take care of him.

To lighten the mood, Spence joked, "I don't know what you're worried about. You're not going to be here."

Still, Spence said he and his mother both were clinging to the tiniest glimmer of hope that she might enjoy another revival, just as she had during the Hawaii trip.

That optimism was reflected in a note to Mary Fischer. With penmanship in an unsteady hand, Mary Jo had written: "Looking forward to a little brighter '11 and more lunches together." But that's not what happened.

Nancy Sholder was puzzled.

She had just returned home from the grocery store. She was listening to a phone message from Robbie Cropper: "Can you call me? Mary Jo wants to talk to you." The message seemed odd. Nancy couldn't think of another time when Robbie had called her during her nineteen-year friendship with Mary Jo Cropper.

Nancy was one of the two women who comforted Mary Jo right after she was first diagnosed with cancer in 1992. She and Mary Jo had worked side-by-side to help others in the Lebanon Presbyterian Church Cancer Support Group. They also had worked together to pull off the successful 2000 Relay for Life fundraiser for the American Cancer Society.

It was now January 2011. When Nancy returned Robbie's call, he didn't bother with chit-chat. He said: "Mary Jo wants to talk to you about whether it would be time to call hospice. Do you think you can come over?" Nancy hated hearing those words. But because she had helped so many other people in the twilight of their lives, she was confident she could also assist Mary Jo—as hard as that would be. "I'll be there in an hour," Nancy told Robbie.

Robbie directed Nancy to a bedroom where she would find Mary Jo. Gingerly, Nancy entered. "She was lying there in a beautiful dark purple robe—thin, but alert. I got down on my knees, and just looked at her face so she could see me," Nancy said.

Mary Jo slowly forced out the words, "I'm not doing well." Her voice was barely above a whisper. Was she in pain? Yes, she said. The medicine wasn't working. Nancy told her that hospice could help with that.

Then came the hardest question: "I asked her if she was afraid to die, and she said, 'No, I just don't want to leave my family.'"

Almost nine years later, while telling that part of the story, Nancy's voice cracked. And she wept as she continued the story: "I hugged her. I kissed her. I told her I loved her. We both were a little tearful, but we didn't sob. She wasn't afraid of leaving; she was sad about leaving."

Nancy had probably spent only ten minutes with Mary Jo. She got Mary Jo's permission to tell Robbie what they had discussed. "I went into the den and sat down with him and told him, 'She knows it's time to have extra support, not only for her, but also for you and Spence and Amy,'" Nancy said. "He was not surprised."

Nancy sent a message via the Facebook social media network to Mary Jo's niece, Cathy Chasteen, on January 9, 2011, reporting on Mary Jo's status: "My heart grieves for her and all of your family … my prayer is that she will have all that she needs to keep her comfortable, and that she can have her loved ones near and will slip into the arms of angels who will carry her home to God."

In late January 2011, the day before Mary Jo was taken to Hospice of Cincinnati in Blue Ash, her daughter, Amy, crawled into bed next to her mother and told her: "I love you. It's OK to let go. We want you to be at peace; we love you. Go."

Mary Jo had wanted to pass away at home. But Robbie had experienced a cascade of health problems after the 2004 auto accident, and he was unable to provide the care his wife needed.

Nancy chose not to visit Mary Jo at Hospice. She wanted to give the family space. "I just thought it was a very private time," she said.

Before Mary Jo entered Hospice, Martie Mehallis made her way up from Florida to spend a final few moments with her life-long friend.

Robbie laid down the law, telling Martie that the visit needed to be limited to twenty minutes. He thought that was all Mary Jo could handle. Especially from vivacious Martie.

She entered the room, gave Mary Jo a hug and a kiss and told her she loved her. As Mary Jo sat in bed, with pillows at her back for comfort, Martie took a seat in a chair beside her. "Then we laughed, told lies and swore like longshoremen," Martie said. "And I told her I had to leave. And she said, 'You're not leaving; you're not leaving. I'm not tired. Just sit down. Don't leave me.'"

So, they continued to talk. Martie noticed a half-dozen boxes of notecards strewn across the bed, within Mary Jo's reach—and she realized that her friend was using the last bits of strength she had, trying to produce her usual torrent of personal notes. "Even when she felt lousy, she would make sure someone else knew she was thinking of them with a phone call or a note or a gift," Martie said. "In fact, I'm sure the post office avoided bankruptcy by keeping her in postage stamps."

Finally, more than an hour had passed, and Martie said, with playful candor that only a close friend would understand, "I see you're getting tired; you're acting stupid now."

The moment they dreaded had arrived. Martie knew she had to leave. "So, I said to her, 'This is it. And I love you.' And we hung on for quite a while. Then I left," Martie said. "I knew it was the last time I would see her."

Reflecting on that day, Martie, rarely at a loss for words, had a hard time talking. But she did articulate how that day reinforced one trait she really appreciated about Mary Jo: How authentically she expressed her feelings.

"At the end of every phone call, every letter, every visit, she would always say, 'I love you.' I knew that my mother loved me, but I don't know that she ever told me that she loved me the way Mary Jo did. It was just so heartfelt," Martie said. "You knew that she meant it—and that she was grateful for your friendship, for your company."

Friends forever, Martie Mehallis and Mary Jo, pictured in a photo that was put on display in the Norris Lake house where Mary Jo sought refuge from cancer.

And Martie knew that, once Mary Jo had passed, no truer friend would ever cross her path again.

In hospice care, Mary Jo was mostly semiconscious and not really responsive. She was being given a lot of sedatives and pain medications. But her loved ones had been told that she could still hear and comprehend what was being said. So they would hold her hand, talk to her, just be by her side—for hours on end.

Among the daily visitors was Susan Weinberg. "She came over every single day on her lunch break or dinner break to come see Mom," Spence said. Those actions spoke volumes to Mary Jo's family, considering how demanding Susan's schedule was as the co-director of the Center. Spence said Susan would say, "She's not my patient. She's my friend." Spence isn't sure that his mom fully grasped how important she was to Susan. Two other Bethesda friends accompanied Susan on one of those final visits: fundraiser Mary Fischer and surgeon Ching Ho.

One by one, others said their goodbyes. Ginny remembers how peaceful Mary Jo looked when she last saw her. Her nails were painted red; so were her lips. "She just looked so pretty, even though she didn't respond," Ginny said.

Clint Dameron, a man who had known Mary Jo since he was a 1-year-old neighbor boy in Centerville, Ohio, was living all the way across the country, in Oregon, when he got word that Mary Jo was at Hospice. He was unable to come and deliver a message in person. So, Clint emailed Spence, his close lifelong friend, asking him to deliver a message to Mary Jo. "It was hard putting anything into words, and one of the hardest things I have ever had to do," Clint told Spence. Mary Jo had been like a mom to Clint. He wrote: "I'd like to think you have done more for me over the last forty years than anyone else. But I wouldn't be surprised in the least to find you had done as much for many others."

Clint thanked Mary Jo for countless dinners, for making sure he went to church; for taking him on family vacations and to Ohio State games. "Your unbridled optimism in light of your own problems and challenges always served to cheer me up and not let me quit when I didn't have a lot of hope," he said. "I am a better person for having had you in my life and wouldn't trade it for anything."

Spence was so emotional, he had to force out the words when reciting Clint's letter to his mom. He hoped she understood what he was saying.

Just a couple days after that, on a cold Sunday afternoon, Mary Jo was surrounded by the warmth of her family members. Her sister, Gail Norris, said, "You could tell she wasn't in pain; she was peaceful."

Medical staff reported that Mary Jo's vital signs were good, so her relatives left for the evening.

And right afterward, Mary Jo's tired body surrendered. She took her last breath. Her heartbeat ceased. And her soul drifted into immortality—a transition that her son sensed very powerfully that night.

It was January 23, 2011, and Mary Jo's husband, Robbie, had received the death-notification call from Hospice. He relayed the news to Spence. "He called me and said, 'Your mom passed away.' Dad was very businesslike," Spence said. "He said all the arrangements had already been made." Although everyone felt incredibly sad, there also was a feeling of relief. "That weight is off, that we don't have to see her suffer anymore," Spence said. Mary Jo had hung on in Hospice for five days, long enough to allow visits from everyone she held dearest.

That night, as Spence lay down to sleep, he noticed a powerful scent wafting past him. "A smell, plain as day, came across my nose. It was a super-strong perfume," Spence said. But it wasn't a scent he could readily identify. Then, Spence felt "this super sense of calm," and sensed the presence of his mother.

"It was a feeling of, 'I'm leaving but this isn't the last time you're going to see me,'" Spence said.

Dana, his wife, said, "It was like she was stopping by, on her way to Heaven."

Months later, while sorting through some of his mother's belongings, Spence ran across a bottle of perfume by designer Alfred Sung. Curious about how it smelled, Spence and Dana spritzed it into the air—and Spence immediately recognized the blend of floral and citrus. It was the same scent that had washed over him the night of his mother's passing—and it was the only perfume that Mary Jo had used for quite a few years.

Spence has faith in eternal life. But this was one of the most amazing validations of that belief he could ever imagine. Especially because his sister, Amy, also had a similar experience. A couple weeks after Mary Jo's death, Amy noticed her mother's special scent filling her car while she drove along roads near the old SanMarGale farm. "I honestly remember having such a calming feel of Mom's presence at that moment," Amy said.

Mary Jo, a woman who had overcome her fear of flying and her fear of dying, had left her children a convincing sign to reassure them that, yes, she had reached her final destination safely. She was soaring among the angels. Forever.

10

Shining Brightly After All

Everything was awash in white. The linens that covered ten round tables for guests to cluster around, plus rectangular tables for food and drink. The napkins, the plates, the coffee cups. And gracing the tables: fourteen dozen white roses in clear glass vases.

Symbols of purity and joy, white roses had been among Mary Jo's favorite flowers since she was a little girl. As she contemplated her final arrangements, Mary Jo selected those flowers to create an atmosphere of peace, light and spirituality. That's what she wanted people to feel when they gathered for her memorial service at Lebanon Presbyterian Church.

On this day, January 28, 2011, Mary Jo's physical presence would make one last stop at the church, which had been her spiritual home. It was where she attended services regularly and served as an elder even when she was ill. It was where she had been married, witnessed her children's baptisms and marriages, mourned her father's passing and uplifted members of the cancer support group.

At age 69, Mary Jo had lived almost one-third of her years under the cloud of cancer. Finally, it had lifted. Now, five days after Mary Jo's death, about four hundred people came to share food and fellowship—and to rejoice in a life that had been well-lived, earning passage into a glorious afterlife.

Mary Jo's close friend, Martie Mehallis, remembers surveying the sea of faces. "I looked out at the congregation," Martie said, "and wondered how many of those people had received a note in that unreadable back-handed writing of hers." Martie loved that long-running joke about Mary Jo's left-handed penmanship. Such happy thoughts commingled with deep pangs of grief and longing as everyone prepared to say goodbye to Mary Jo Stolle Cropper for the last time.

Every detail turned out just as she had planned. "Mary Jo was not often a take-charge person," Martie said. "But this time, with her funeral, she sure was."

Per Mary Jo's request, church ladies had baked batches of the sour cream coffeecake perfected

A dove soars in a stained-glass window at Lebanon Presbyterian Church, the center of Mary Jo's spiritual life.

by Mary Jo's mother, Dorothy Stolle. That was one of the cherished recipes included in Mary Jo's Stolle/Cropper cookbook. It was a comfort food. Mary Jo hoped the special recipe would uplift sad faces and would help people feel a little extra love as they savored its sugary-cinnamon goodness. Other refreshments included fresh fruit, muffins, mini quiches, water and juice, along with hot coffee and tea to take off the winter chill.

As guests arrived, greeters directed them to mingle in the multipurpose room where the tables were set up. Then ushers took groups into the nearby narthex to greet Mary Jo's family. Finally, those who were staying for the service would be guided to take seats in the sanctuary. "She had all of this set up so that everybody would be relaxed and would be able to visit with family in a very organized way," Brenda Bingham, the church secretary, said. "She wanted everyone to feel loved and cared for, and not put pressure on her family. She told me, 'I don't want them to have to worry about anything.'"

Thus, Brenda said, "Her family got to just be with the guests who came in. They were able to just share time with each other—to share the moment, just be in the moment."

Months in advance, all of those plans had been finalized, Brenda said: "At that point, we were just waiting. We had all these plans ready to go when the time came."

And when the church's pastor, the Rev. Peter Larson, contacted Brenda at home to tell her that Mary Jo had died on January 23, 2011, Brenda felt a mixture of sadness and relief. Brenda remembers thinking: "She's whole again. She's in Heaven."

Then Brenda cried. "She was just such a wonderful lady," Brenda said, "and she was going to be someone who everyone would miss." Including Brenda. "I just really looked up to her," Brenda said. "She was a fighter, and she had faith and believed in God until the end."

As the service began with a gentle piano melody, the man sitting at the keyboard tried to imagine he was somewhere else. That's how pianist Jay Mills always copes when he plays at a funeral. Jay is a sentimental guy, and that is the only way he can tamp down his emotions enough to play piano for people mourning a loss. That was especially true at Mary Jo's service, because Jay felt such a personal connection to her.

Jay and Mary Jo had been acquainted a long time, and every interaction had been so delightful, steeped in music and merriment. But Jay thinks Mary Jo may not have known how special she was to him. Jay also thinks Mary Jo may have been unaware that his first memory of her dated back to his boyhood—nearly five decades before she enlisted him to play soothing music during her memorial service.

In the 1960s, when Jay was a student at Louisa Wright Elementary School in Lebanon, Ohio, "I just remember going home and saying, 'We had a really nice lady as our substitute today,'" Jay said. Although substitute teachers come and go, Jay sensed something extraordinary about Mary Jo. She had a sparkle that made her stand out more than the average substitute. He even recalls exactly what she was wearing: A nice plaid skirt, possibly a Pendleton. And a white, long-sleeved blouse with ruffles on the collar and cuffs. "I remember it like it was yesterday," he said during an interview in 2020. Some ladies who are stylish and immaculately groomed can seem standoffish, but not Mary Jo. She seemed so approachable, so affable, Jay said.

In his adulthood, Jay was thrilled to reconnect with that charming substitute teacher. But Jay was unsure whether he and Mary Jo ever discussed his first memory of her from so long ago.

When Jay played piano at various venues, he would often see Mary Jo and Robbie Cropper. One frequent place was the Black Horse Tavern inside Lebanon's historic Golden Lamb Inn & Restaurant, one of Mary Jo's hangouts. Jay has had a standing gig there for quite a while.

"Wherever I was, she would try to sit at a table close to where I was playing," Jay said. Sometimes, Jay and Mary Jo would get a chance to chat. He found those conversations "uplifting." And she always expressed appreciation for his talent, with her words and actions. "As she left, she would put her hand on my face, pat my face and tell me I did a wonderful job," Jay said. Then she would leave a tip—a generous one. If Jay had to leave before Mary Jo did, he would always go to her and say goodbye.

Jay also was among the legions who had received cards and notes from Mary Jo.

After Mary Jo told him that she had cancer, Jay sometimes noticed Mary Jo wearing a wig, perhaps even a blond one; he knew that was because chemotherapy had made her hair fall out. Other times, Mary Jo would be absent, and Robbie would come up to Jay and say, "Hello," and "Sorry she's not here because she's not feeling well."

Then, all of a sudden, Jay learned Mary Jo was gravely ill. Then Jay got word that he was being enlisted to play piano at her memorial service, which could happen in short order. While Jay was flattered that Mary Jo had chosen him, he sadly waited for the day when he would need to fulfill that final request. "I got home one day, and Pastor Larson had called and left a message— and my heart dropped," Jay said, "because I knew why he was calling; he would not have another reason to call me."

Jay considered it "an honor and a privilege to have known her," and to have been selected to provide music for her service. "And for months and months afterward, someone would talk about her, and it would just bring tears to my eyes," Jay said, "because I had such regard for her." Almost a decade after Jay's last notes rang in the air at Mary Jo's service, people still would occasionally tell him: "You did such a great job for her."

As Mary Jo requested, Jay launched the service by playing two selections. One was *I'll Walk with God*. That tune was new to Jay even though he had been playing piano for more than 50 years by then. Part of the lyrics seemed to convey a message from Mary Jo: "I'll walk with God from this day on.... There is no death though eyes grow dim; There is no fear when I'm near to Him."

Mary Jo's service also honored her deceased parents. The comforting 23rd Psalm was read in memory of her mother; a hymn, *Seek Ye First the Kingdom of God,* was sung on behalf of her father, Ralph Stolle.

In hopes of consoling people who had gathered, Mary Jo enlisted friends to recite short passages from The Bible. Martie read a section of John 14, in which Jesus admonished His disciples, "Do not let your hearts be troubled.... My Father's house has many rooms.... You know the way to the place where I am going." Nan Sempsrott, the friend whose breast cancer first put Mary Jo in contact with the original Bethesda breast center in 2005, read from Psalm 16: "My heart is glad, and my tongue rejoices; my body also will rest secure."

Then it was time for the Rev. Alice Petersen, who had also fought breast cancer and was recruited for the first Wahines trip to Hawaii, to read something that had deeply touched Mary Jo's heart: The speech her son, Spence, had given at the Center's Grand Opening sixteen months earlier.

Next came remarks from the doctor whose dream Mary Jo shared, Susan Weinberg. After Mary Jo decided to make her large contribution to the Center, "her commitment began our partnership, which led to a wonderful friendship," Susan said.

"I learned a lot from my friend, Mary Jo, by watching how she lived," Susan said. "Mary Jo showed me how to use each day to show those around her how much she cared about them."

Susan cited a personal example. In early January 2011, just as Mary Jo's health took a major turn for the worse, Susan's father became critically ill. This was just a couple weeks before Mary Jo died. Yet, "when she was so sick, I received notes from her inquiring about my father's circumstance," Susan said. When Mary Jo felt too weak to write, she would call to check on Susan and her dad. "This is compassion; this is caring," Susan said.

"Mary Jo taught me that we should strive at all costs to make a better world, so that, someday, if we have the chance to look back on our time here, we can know we spent it well, that we have made a difference," Susan said. "This is Mary Jo's legacy: She has left the world a better place for those forty-five thousand women we serve in her Center." The number of patients visiting the Center would continue to grow.

When it came time for Pastor Peter Larson to preach, he reflected on how much it helped everyone that Mary Jo had planned her entire service, from beginning to end. He looked at the crowd overflowing the sanctuary. It was the largest attendance at a memorial service since Peter had become the church's pastor almost eight years earlier. "I don't think they were there because she was the daughter of Ralph Stolle," Peter said later. "I think it was because of all the lives she had touched personally."

Then Peter recounted instances of Mary Jo's kindness. He also quoted some of Mary Jo's own words. This part of the sermon stayed with some of Mary Jo's relatives for nearly a decade; they were touched to hear the words she had written almost exactly a year before she died.

In an email written on Monday, January 25, 2010, Mary Jo told Peter that his Sunday sermon made her mull over her journey with cancer. "I think it's very natural, early on, to think, 'Why me?' I remember someone saying to me, 'Why NOT me?' I decided to not dwell on the 'whys' but hopefully, to grow to be a stronger person. My situation wasn't going to change. So that meant my attitude needed to change to provide me the peace I felt would allow me to look at each and every day as a gift."

The email continued: "I think, for the first time ever, I just totally said, 'God, show me how to be strong and show me how to help others live their life to the fullest with a disease I know a

This sanctuary at Lebanon Presbyterian Church was overflowing with people who came to say goodbye to Mary Jo Cropper in 2011.

little bit about and can relate to. You've got to help me because I can't do it on my own.'"

Mary Jo's email concluded: "Now, with more and more of our congregation being diagnosed with serious illnesses, it's so important they know: This is not a punishment, but a gift. Once they understand that, they will know what to do with that gift."

Those words expanded upon a theme that Mary Jo had shared with Ginny Kuntz, her sister-in-law. "She would say 'Cancer is a gift,' and I'd tell her, 'What? You've got to be kidding me!'" Ginny said. And then, Ginny said, Mary Jo would explain, "No, really, it is. It's brought me out of my shell." Mary Jo was proud of setting aside her public-speaking jitters and accepting invitations to tell groups of women about her cancer battle, Ginny said. On one occasion, Mary Jo even addressed a group of frightened high school girls, whose soccer teammate was diagnosed with breast cancer. "They were just sitting with wide eyes, on the edge of their seat," as Mary Jo spoke, said church secretary Brenda Bingham, whose husband had coached that team. Mary Jo and Susan Weinberg arranged a tour of the Center for those girls, Brenda said.

Dana Cropper, Mary Jo's daughter-in-law, thinks cancer drew Mary Jo closer to God. "She believed God always had a plan for her, and I think she realized that when she got cancer, it was that she was meant to touch other people's lives, to be a light of encouragement," Dana said. Whether a friend, a relative or a stranger, "I don't think she would ever want anyone to feel like they were alone in their fight. And that's where her faith comes in, too," Dana said. "With Jesus, you are not alone."

You'll Never Walk Alone was one of the songs Mary Jo chose for her service.

Mary Jo's religious faith was paramount, followed closely by her love of family, friends, students—and of The Ohio State University. That's why no service for Mary Jo would have been complete without a few references to her beloved alma mater.

At one point, Pastor Larson joked, "When we were planning this memorial service, Mary Jo told me that she expected *all* of you today would be dressed in scarlet and gray," OSU's colors. The service ended with *Carmen Ohio*, an early 1900s anthem that is still sung after OSU home games. It was one of the few things that would bring Mary Jo's husband, Robbie, to tears. The song begins: "Oh come let's sing Ohio's praise ... the seasons pass, the years will roll." It ends with "O-hi-o!"

With that, Mary Jo's casket was carried out of the sanctuary and back into the atrium, where it had been positioned during the two-hour visitation.

Afterward, Mary Jo's guests headed for a reception that she intended as a true celebration of her life.

Pam Hatfield Russell walked away from the service feeling like she had witnessed something special. Pam had only seen Mary Jo occasionally since the early 1990s, when Mary Jo last taught alongside her in the Lebanon schools. Still, Pam wanted to attend the service out of respect for Mary Jo. And Pam's daughter, Katie, wanted to go and support her friend, Mary Jo's granddaughter, Josie Cropper. When she heard that Mary Jo had pre-planned the entire service, Pam was impressed—but not really surprised. "It was Mary Jo's way," Pam said. "She had it down to every last little detail."

Pam wasn't sure whether she and her daughter should go to the post-service reception at The River's Bend country club, near Mary Jo and Robbie's home. "They said everyone was invited, but I felt like it wasn't my place. I'm not family," Pam said. "But I'm so glad I went, because it was such a tribute to Mary Jo. Just with everyone talking, having food and drinks, it was definitely upbeat. And that was the way I was told she wanted it."

Meanwhile, back at the church, Pastor Peter Larson was all alone. He felt drawn to pay his respects one final time, in private, to this woman who was clearly so Christ-centered. Peter thought about all the gifts, large and small, that she and her husband, Robbie, had given to people in the church and to the church itself. He remembered how, when the church needed to raise $3.6 million for an expansion, the Croppers stepped up with a five-figure contribution. "And, it was so low-key, no strings attached," he would recount later. "Sometimes people who make that kind of contribution want something, like a plaque or whatever. But they didn't want anything."

Mary Jo was among a rare breed of givers: the quiet, humble, anonymous ones. Just as stated in Matthew 6: "When you give to the needy, do not sound a trumpet before you … do not let your left hand know what your right hand is doing, so that your giving may be in secret. And your Father, who sees what is done in secret, will reward you."

In the atrium, natural light pours through skylights, illuminating the room even on an overcast day, as it was that Friday afternoon. Mary Jo's casket was positioned beneath a cross made of stained glass, mostly light blue. Peter thought about Mary Jo's personalized approach to charity. "The creative part," Peter said, "was her thinking about: 'How can I be the light?'"

Earlier that day, in his sermon, Peter had pointed out that many people come to a point in life when they have a "cross" to bear: cancer, another serious illness or some situation that causes pain and suffering. "We can sit there and focus on our pain and suffering—or we can DENY ourselves and pick up that cross and follow Jesus." That is what Mary Jo did, Peter told the mourners.

Now, after everyone had left the church, Peter walked up and took one last look at Mary Jo. "And nearly the same words that the angels spoke to the women at Jesus' tomb came to me: 'She is not here; she is risen,'" Peter said. "Somehow, those words were just impressed in my heart at that moment. It was so obvious that she wasn't in that cancer-ridden body anymore."

Mary Jo's soul had ascended to a place alongside Ralph and Dorothy Stolle, cousin Frieda Pirmann and other dearly departed loved ones. Now they were looking down from above. Or, as expressed in an old Eskimo proverb, printed on the back cover of Mary Jo's memorial program: "Perhaps they are not stars, but rather openings in Heaven, where the love of our lost ones pours through and shines down upon us to let us know they are happy."

That night, after Mary Jo's service, the sky surely was twinkling more brightly.

Epilogue

In some ways, Mary Jo Cropper became more powerful after her death.

By 2019, sixty thousand patients a year were using the Center that bears her name, fifteen thousand more patients than when it opened a decade earlier. A fundraising gala for the Center, held each year since Mary Jo's death in 2011, raised a total of $3.3 million. And all of TriHealth benefited from synergy that the Cropper Center ignited.

"Mary Jo had no idea what she was creating, and what has been reproduced from her single act of generosity. I don't think any of us did," said Jamie Easterling, who helped launch the Center before he became president of TriHealth's Good Samaritan Hospital. "What we have created, I believe, is absolutely priceless."

The Center challenged the status quo at TriHealth. Some people had questioned the need for a separate breast center, Jamie said, because they were stuck in a mindset of: "This is the way we've always done it." They were afraid to change. But after people saw the Center's success—and the way it revolutionized the experience for patients—more patient-focused changes picked up momentum throughout the TriHealth system, Jamie said.

With that in mind, TriHealth completed an $80-million expansion on the Bethesda North campus. The lead donors, Harold M. Thomas and his wife, Eugenia S. Thomas, contributed $10 million toward that project. Mr. Thomas and his now-deceased wife, Margret, had made large contributions to the Cropper Center previously.

In early 2020, the Cropper Center retained its name and moved into the second floor of the three-story Thomas Comprehensive Care Center. The impressive structure spans 140,000 square feet.

"To me, the Mary Jo Cropper Family Center for Breast Care was the starting point for all of that," said Regina Eaton, a long-time assistant to the Cropper Center's co-director, Dr. Susan Weinberg. Both Regina and Susan retired before the Thomas Center opened.

Under a single roof, the Thomas Center encompasses testing, surgery and treatment services for people with lung, heart, circulation or breast issues, plus all types of cancer. It also offers screenings to ensure that healthy people stay that way.

"If a person is diagnosed with a problem, whatever that is, that person will know: Everything is going to be taken care of, from that point forward," Regina said. "That's what Dr. Weinberg and Mary Jo and all the employees wanted for the Center's patients—coordinated care all the way through, so the patients at least don't have to worry about that."

Mary Jo's daughter, Amy Cropper Winkler, was among one hundred honored guests who attended a ribbon-cutting for the new Thomas Center in January 2020, a week before the ninth anniversary of her mother's death. After touring the new Cropper Center there, Amy said: "Mom would be beyond thrilled with that new building."

"Mom was all about making things easier for the patient, and she would love knowing that it's all in one spot now," Amy said. Located only a few hundred yards from the original Cropper Center, the new Thomas Center echoes features that helped make the Cropper Center special, including a loop-shaped staircase and some artwork from the former Cropper building. Also, abundant natural light fills the Thomas Center's glass-walled entrance, nourishing two thousand live tropical plants in a vertical garden that is fifty feet tall—a spectacular first impression.

Inside the Thomas Center, the relocated Cropper Center is equipped with state-of-the-art technology; it has upgraded all of its mammography equipment to provide 3-D imaging, said Jacqui Appel, who became breast program manager for all of Tri-Health. Jacqui explained that 3-D mammography takes multiple

A keepsake box, lovingly decorated by Mary Jo's first grandchild, Ali Settlemyre, holds photos and other treasured mementoes.

X-ray images of the breast, creating a three-dimensional view of the tissue. Traditional mammograms take one picture at a time. The 3-D images reveal far more detail and can help detect cancer sooner, Jacqui said. Another advantage: fewer patients needing to be asked to return for additional imaging.

In 2011, two years after it opened in its original location, the Cropper Center became the first Cincinnati-area facility to offer 3-D mammography to the general public, Jacqui said. Now, in its new location, the Cropper Center has six mammography rooms and three ultrasound rooms dedicated to breast imaging. Breast MRI images also can be obtained in the Thomas Center. In addition, bone-density scans are offered to make sure that older patients, or those undergoing chemotherapy, aren't developing osteoporosis, or brittle bones.

Outside, thirteen thousand plants fill the landscape; at the front entry, Gail Stolle Norris and Sandra Stolle Perry dedicated a garden to their parents, Ralph and Dorothy Stolle, and to their sister, Mary Jo Stolle Cropper.

Mary Jo's son, Spence, thinks the chain reaction that continued after his mother's death would have dazzled her. "Her million-dollar investment has paid dividends far beyond anything she ever would have expected," Spence said. "I wish she could have seen the return on her investment. She would just be in awe."

Mary Jo had invested in the future of thousands of people, including some who were dear to her—several of whom would later benefit from the Center in ways that she hoped would never be necessary.

Shortly after Mary Jo died, supporters came up with a special way to honor her—and to raise funds. They started an annual event called "Mary Jo's Angels," to be held in or around October, National Breast Cancer Awareness Month. For people who are familiar with the angel smiley-face that Mary Jo often scrawled with her signature on notecards, the name seems especially apropos. The award recognizes people who acted like "angels" in the fight against cancer.

Among the first to be named an Angel was Nancy Sholder, the nurse and lay minister who had comforted Mary Jo at the beginning of her cancer journey—and at the end.

Nancy was notified about the Angels honor on September 27, 2011—a date significant to her in more ways than one. On that date, Mary Fischer from the Bethesda Foundation was calling. She told Nancy something like this: "Congratulations, you've been selected as one of Mary Jo's Angels!" Mary briefly explained the award, then Nancy blurted out, "You're not going to believe this, but I know I have breast cancer. I saw it this morning."

Nancy had just undergone an ultrasound of her left breast at another medical facility, not the Cropper Center. Nancy had glanced at a monitor. "And I saw the cancer," Nancy said. Because Nancy was a nurse and had medical knowledge, she *knew* it was malignant, even though there was no official confirmation yet.

Nancy explained this to Mary, whom she had never met. "And being the professional that she was, Mary said, 'If there's any way we can be of extra support to you, call me,'" Nancy recalled.

Nancy was having trouble getting a biopsy scheduled through the other healthcare provider. She turned to Mary for help. "Within minutes, Mary called me back and said, 'You're to call Dr. Weinberg tonight at eight o'clock, after she completes her duties in the emergency department,'" Nancy said. During that conversation, Dr. Weinberg told Nancy she would meet her at the Bethesda North lobby the next morning, and to bring her reports and CDs of her images. Nancy said Dr. Weinberg confirmed Nancy's fears were on target: She *did* have breast cancer, but doctors needed to get a tissue sample to figure out what type. Dr. Weinberg directed Nancy to meet Dr. Anthony Antonoplos at the Cropper Center for that procedure.

Afterward, as Dr. Antonoplos washed his hands, "I started to have a meltdown," Nancy said. "I was holding it in—and it all came out. He patted me on the shoulder and said, 'We are going to take the best care of you.'"

Eight years later, as Nancy recounted the story, the doctor's compassion still touched her. "A lot of doctors would have dashed out the door, away from this crying woman," Nancy said. "But for him to stand there and do that was just so reassuring."

Nancy was stunned by the turn of events. She had no risk factors, other than being female and age 70; she never thought breast cancer would affect her. When it did, Nancy silently thanked her friend, Mary Jo: "From the moment I walked through the door of that breast center, I just felt like Mary Jo was right there on my shoulder."

The next day, Nancy was notified that her type of cancer required surgery, and she was given an appointment time for that. She ended up having a mastectomy—and the surgeon discovered several lymph nodes were positive for cancer, too. As a result, Nancy had to undergo six rounds of chemo and twenty-four radiation treatments.

Still, that November 9th, three weeks after her surgery, Nancy attended the Angels event at the Manor House, a banquet hall in Mason, Ohio. "Because of Mary Jo, I ended up at the best possible place for cancer treatment," Nancy said, "and that phone call that Mary Fischer made to me, telling me I was a Mary Jo's Angel, changed everything."

Nancy said she knew little about the Cropper Center until she became a patient there. "Mary Jo didn't talk about what she was giving to other people. So I didn't know about it for a time," Nancy said. "I don't remember how I found out about it, and her role in it, but it wasn't from her."

Cancer came back in Nancy's other breast just two years later, in 2013, leading to her second mastectomy. However, that course of treatment was much easier than it was during her first go-round. As of early 2020, there was no sign of a recurrence; sadly, the other woman who had helped Nancy comfort Mary Jo upon her original diagnosis, Jean Sidebottom, passed away in 2019. Jean had struggled with a number of health issues, including breast cancer, Nancy said.

Although Nancy was honored to be chosen as one of Mary Jo's Angels, she thinks that Dr. Susan Weinberg and Mary Jo became *her* angels. "When I look back on everything, I'm just so thankful for Dr. Weinberg," she said. "And I'm so grateful that Mary Jo was so generous, starting that Center that ended up helping me personally and thousands of other women."

Thinking about the connection between Mary Jo and Susan Weinberg, Nancy recalled Susan's remarks at Mary Jo's memorial service. "What I remember, especially with fondness, was the way Dr. Weinberg spoke about Mary Jo," Nancy said. "She spoke about the legacy that she left to women. About the kindness that Mary Jo showed to everyone in making the breast center happen, and about their relationship with each other and how much they cared for one another."

The first Angels gala, where Nancy was an Angel award recipient, drew almost four hundred people and raised more than $215,000; the event has remained popular and financially successful ever since. Each year, money raised at the gala is earmarked for special purposes, including clinical research. In early 2020, special touches were in the works for the tenth annual Celebration of Angels gala in October.

A longtime friend of the Cropper-Stolle family, Bill Falknor, said, "I'm always amazed at the level of participation in the gala—law firms, banks, all sorts of companies.... Mary Jo's been gone now quite a few years, and everybody still participates. I think that says something about the cause and about her."

The Angels celebration helped put salve on the wounds of those closest to Mary Jo, as did the continued success of the Cropper Center.

Still, grief has a strange way of sneaking up and biting hard when folks least expect it. In the coming months and years, Mary Jo's family would weather trying times. Some of those difficult situations had nothing to do with her death. Others had everything to do with it.

For a whole year after Mary Jo died, her devoted sister-in-law, Ginny Kuntz, said she couldn't stop asking herself: "How am I gonna make it?"

The second year, Ginny kept expecting Mary Jo to walk through the door, with her distinctive gait and posture. She was mildly bow-legged, and her neck was usually craned slightly forward. Ginny misses that. Ginny misses everything about Mary Jo.

Ginny kept flashing back to one of her last memories of Mary Jo before she went into hospice care. It was around Christmastime 2010, a few weeks before Mary Jo would pass away. Ginny had driven to Mary Jo's house to drop off something. She noticed Mary Jo was keeping watch while her dog, a Welsh terrier named Sadie, went outside. "I can still see her in the dark and the snow, with the light on the back porch, just a pretty silhouette with her in her robe, being with the animal she loved," Ginny said. She didn't have the heart to bother Mary Jo, so Ginny quietly placed her delivery on the stoop and drove away, misty-eyed.

After Mary Jo died, Ginny's brother, Robbie, started to quickly deteriorate.

The entire family was worried about Robbie; they spent extra time with him. For a short time, while their new home was being built, Spence and his family moved in with Robbie. And everyone tried to include him in activities. But Robbie just seemed to lack the same vigor and zest for life that he once had.

"When Mom passed away, it was like part of him passed away," said the Croppers' daughter, Amy. "He would still do things. But his whole demeanor was very lonely, very withdrawn.

When Mary Jo's husband, Robbie Cropper, passed away in 2018, the family took comfort in knowing that he was reunited with Mary Jo.

You could just tell he seemed lost without her. She was the glue that held the family together."

While Mary Jo was still alive, Robbie was already suffering significant health issues. In February 2008, while Mary Jo was gone on the Buckeye Cruise for Cancer, Robbie called Ginny at 4 a.m. Robbie told her that he had spent the night on the floor after his back had given out. An ambulance was on its way to take him to Bethesda North. Robbie was diagnosed with spinal stenosis, a degenerative bone disease.

One thing after another seemed to happen to him after his wife died in 2011. Robbie knew he was slipping away. At one point, when the family dog had to be euthanized, Robbie's granddaughters had volunteered to pool their money to buy another dog to keep Robbie company. "The girls' offer touched his heart, but he turned it down," Ginny said, adding that her brother had declared: "I appreciate it, but I'll die before the new dog would."

Robbie's left leg never completely healed after the 2004 car accident, Ginny said. The leg kept getting infected and it didn't get proper blood flow. Finally, doctors had to amputate the leg in July 2017. Ginny would take Robbie to physical therapy appointments, "and those would wear him out," Ginny said. "It was good to see him upright, walking, but I felt sorry for him because it was such hard work."

Ginny and Robbie's parents had both passed away in the month of April, so sister and brother would kid each other, "Well, we made it through another April!" But Ginny had a premonition that her brother wouldn't make it through another April. And he didn't.

On April 11, 2018, Robbie succumbed to kidney failure. He was 77.

Robbie's death hit everyone hard, but the family did take some comfort in picturing him reunited with Mary Jo. Once, as the family was visiting Mary Jo's gravesite, Ginny noticed her brother leaning against his car; he seemed to be deep in thought. When she asked what was on his mind, he replied: "I'm going over my list … the list of everything she wanted me to do after she died."

After Robbie passed away, the family held a private graveside service before he was laid to rest next to Mary Jo. The lead pastor from the Antioch Church, which meets at the Stolle YMCA, David Newman, officiated. He is a close family friend of Robbie's son, Spence, and daughter-in-law, Dana.

At the service, David gave each family member a small wooden cross in memory of Robbie. David explained this was the same type of cross that he had given to Robbie shortly before his death. Ginny still carries one of those crosses in her purse—a reminder of what the minister shared about Robbie's faith in God. Robbie had clung to that cross and told the minister: "Believing in Him was the most important thing."

The passing of Robbie Cropper came at an especially stressful time for his daughter, Amy. After divorcing her children's father, Dale Settlemyre, Amy had found love again. But she was married to Gary Winkler for less than four years when he died of a heart attack. Gary died on December 3, 2017. He was only 45; his death was sudden and unexpected.

And Amy and the rest of her family had also just mourned the loss of Mary Jo's lifelong friend, Nan Lesan Sempsrott—the one whose breast cancer set wheels in motion for Mary Jo to establish the Center. Nan, 75, died on May 13, 2017; a week later, her husband, Herb, died.

That string of losses taught Amy a powerful lesson: "I don't think you appreciate when you are young that there will come a time when members of your family—and people who are important to you—will no longer be there. You just don't think about that."

Still, those loved ones do leave imprints that never vanish. Amy is grateful that her father taught her the value of being quiet and introspective, and that her mother taught her the importance of compassion and love.

And, to this day, Amy draws strength from her mom in many ways. She keeps a special note from Mary Jo, written on cream-colored paper, in her bedside table. Amy refers to it now and then. Amy prefers to keep the contents private, but she said the main message from her mother was: "You will have difficulties in life, but I'll always be there."

When Amy has looked outside her house in recent years, she has often noticed a trio of cardinals. She likes to think that those colorful birds represent the continued presence of three departed loved ones: her mom, her dad and her husband.

After her Auntie Mary died, Cathy Chasteen looked over the course of her life and took stock of how much Mary Jo had supported her and influenced her—much more than the typical aunt probably would. She had no way to foresee a watershed moment that would intensify Mary Jo's influence almost eight years after her death.

One of Cathy's earliest memories of Mary Jo centered around a special Valentine's Day gift. When Cathy was in third grade, Mary Jo had given her a red velvet dress accented with white frills. Cathy thought the dress was irresistibly beautiful. She couldn't wait to wear it the next day. So she *didn't*. "I was so excited that I wore it to bed that night," Cathy said, smiling broadly at the thought, more than five decades later.

Then there was the treasured dictionary Mary Jo had given to her as a high-school graduation gift.

Cathy also felt nostalgic about the old Stolle family reunions, where "everyone always gravitated toward Mary Jo." That was because she always took such interest in what was going on in people's lives, Cathy said.

Then, in the mid-2000s, Cathy had a particularly sentimental experience with Mary Jo and her other aunt, Gail Norris. They presented Cathy with a necklace to cheer her during a rough time in her life. They told her, "We had this necklace made for you from Mother's wedding ring." A thick gold setting encircles a diamond that Cathy's grandpa, Ralph Stolle, had given to his wife, Dorothy, before he became successful.

Cathy was touched to receive that heirloom because she been very close to both grandparents; she often had stayed with Grandma Dorothy while Ralph was out of town. "The necklace takes my breath away," Cathy said. "It's very simple but the meaning it has for me is immeasurable."

Cathy reflected on all of those memories after attending a luncheon that turned out to be a farewell to Mary Jo. No one wanted to say so, but most attendees Mary Jo had invited to her house knew this could be the final time they would gather with her. "We were trying to have a happy ladies' lunch, just talking about everyday things," Cathy said. "Everyone was kind of dancing around the subject: How sick she was, and that we might not have her much longer."

Cathy remembers Mary Jo was thin, but her sense of humor was intact. However, Mary Jo soon got tired and had to go lie down. Cathy realized it was time to say goodbye. She went into Mary Jo's bedroom. In the window beside Mary Jo's bed, Cathy noticed it was snowing lightly. She bent over and kissed Mary Jo's forehead, then said, "I have to go. And I love you." Then she told Mary Jo's daughter, Amy, that she loved her, too.

"And I almost ran out of there," Cathy said. "I just felt like: 'I can't face this.'"

In her private moments, Cathy faced the undeniable truth. She wrote in her journal on January 4, 2011: "My Aunt Mary Jo does not have long to live." And, because of that, Cathy also wrote this: She knew she would need God in her life even more after Mary Jo passed away. Cathy also noted that January 13 would mark the 15-year anniversary of Grandpa Stolle's passing.

Then, on January 23, 2011, Cathy received word of her aunt's death. She thought back to the luncheon. "I don't know if I knew that would be the last time I'd see her," Cathy said. "But it was."

Although everyone knew Mary Jo's death was imminent, the news still felt shocking, Cathy said. She initially felt a sense of injustice. "I kept thinking, 'Of all people, why her?'" Cathy said. She cried at first. Then Cathy had to collect herself so she could notify other relatives.

A few days later, Cathy went to Lebanon Presbyterian Church to ask whether childcare would be available during Auntie Mary's memorial service. Yes, her aunt had planned for that—along with all the other details. "When I heard that, it was like someone sucked the air out of the room," Cathy said. "For her to do that, to have everything planned to a 'T,' was just unbelievably touching."

As Cathy sat at the memorial service, knowing all of it was Mary Jo's doing, everything felt that much more meaningful—and more emotional. Cathy wiped away so many tears, she filled her entire purse with used tissues. "Still can't believe she is gone," Cathy journaled.

The day after the service, on January 29, 2011, the family gathered for a private burial at Lebanon Cemetery. "The day started out with a beautiful sunrise," Cathy noted in her journal. But she also wrote how difficult it was to make "a final goodbye."

In her mind's eye, Cathy pictured the toughest and most joyous times of her life—and Mary Jo was ever-present, as Cathy inscribed in her journal: "She has *always* been there."

Cathy appreciated everything Mary Jo did, even small things such as sending annual birthday cards without fail. Cathy got a kick out of the humorous cards her aunt usually selected. The last one Cathy would receive from Auntie Mary did, in fact, make her laugh. Even though Mary Jo had suffered so much from cancer of the breast, she still was able to see the humor in a breast-themed birthday card. The front of the card shows a cartoon of a saggy-breasted woman holding up a brassiere. And she is asking a store clerk: "Do you have this in a 34-long?" Inside, the message reads: "May your birthday cup runneth over!"

That card arrived in time for Cathy's birthday in February of 2010.

The following year, knowing no birthday card from Auntie Mary would ever come again, Cathy had a dream on Valentine's Day: Mary Jo "was healthy and smiling," her journal said. With that image in mind, the next day, Cathy visited Mary Jo's grave. She left behind some tulips.

To Cathy's surprise, a special piece of mail did arrive on her birthday that year—her fiftieth. It was a note from the Lebanon church pastor, Peter Larson. Cathy saw it as God's way of showing her that Mary Jo was thinking of her that day.

The note acknowledged the thanks that Cathy and her husband, Ron, had expressed for Peter's role in Mary Jo's memorial service. Peter responded: "She was a remarkable woman of God and the light of Christ burned so brightly and purely in her life to the very end ... and will continue to shine more radiantly now in Heaven."

"I visited her grave last week to thank the Lord again for her life," Peter wrote. "I'm sure you must be missing her very much." He closed with references to scriptures about eternal life.

Over the next few years, Mary Jo was never far from Cathy's mind, even though she got busy with a bevy of grandchildren. Cathy, a mother of three, already had four grandchildren while Mary Jo was still alive. Nine more grandbabies came along afterward. And then, on December 3, 2018, about eight months after her thirteenth grandchild was born, Cathy was walloped with terrible news: *She, too, had breast cancer.*

Cathy reacted rather calmly; her response was: "We'll do what we've gotta do." She had already determined: "I'm gonna fight this, because I saw Mary Jo fight it." She felt as if Auntie Mary were right there with her, exerting a calming influence.

Several months earlier, Cathy had noticed a small lump near her left collarbone, "where you normally would put your hand over your heart," Cathy said. Initially, she kept telling herself that the little bump was nothing to worry about. But during this same time, Marsha Falknor, the travel agent and family friend, was going through breast cancer treatment, too. Her cancer had been discovered on Valentine's Day 2018—and hers was more advanced, Stage III. Cathy's, however, was found at Stage I; the diameter of her tumor was only about one centimeter.

Cathy and Marsha could hardly believe that, within a few months of each other, they had both become cancer patients of The Mary Jo Cropper Family Center for Breast Care. While Marsha had been going to the Center for checkups prior to her diagnosis, Cathy had initial tests done at another facility, but turned to the Cropper Center after signs of trouble surfaced. She felt more confident in the care she would receive there.

"When I see Mary Jo's name on the building, I just stop and am so thankful for what she did," Cathy said. She sighs to herself: "Oh, Auntie Mary." And she misses her.

Because Marsha's diagnosis was first—and her cancer was more advanced—she was an inspiration to Cathy. "I knew if Marsha could do it, so could I. I saw her fight and I was ready to fight," Cathy said.

Cathy, then 57, underwent a lumpectomy on New Year's Eve 2018, followed by twelve rounds of chemo and twenty rounds of radiation. Marsha's type of cancer required treatments in a different order. First, large doses of various drugs dissolved the tumor, which preserved Marsha's breast tissue. If that hadn't worked, the tumor was so large, she would have lost her entire breast. After the tumor disintegrated, Marsha had surgery so doctors could make sure that cells surrounding the tumor were cancer-free. Finally, Marsha underwent thirty rounds of radiation.

It was a lot to endure. But Marsha, who was 47 when she was diagnosed, said that her friend and former neighbor, breast cancer survivor Anna Frank, provided valuable perspective. Anna told Marsha that she would go through a terrible time during treatment, "but it's for you to be able to live to be an old woman." Anna was named a Mary Jo's Angel in 2018 for helping Marsha. In early 2020, Marsha was doing well after passing her two-year diagnosis date.

"I wish Mary Jo was still alive, so I could thank her," Marsha said, as she began to cry. "I'm just so thankful for her and for that breast center, because it saved my life. Thank goodness she left us all the breast center."

Marsha said new drugs are better at pinpointing cancer cells and preventing new ones from forming. "If Mary Jo could have had those types of things, she might still be with us," Marsha said.

For both Marsha and Cathy, it's a bit surreal to think they knew the woman whose name is on the building—but they're so glad they did.

"She just had so many wonderful qualities," Marsha said. "She just had this 'aura,' or whatever that word is. You just wanted to be her friend. She just loved to make other people feel good."

Marsha's husband, Bill, said he admired Mary Jo for taking action instead of sitting idly by. "She knew she was going to die of cancer, and that there was no cure. She just could have said, 'The hell with it.' Yet she made the Center possible so that others could live," he said.

As Cathy went through her own cancer treatment, she developed a new appreciation for Mary Jo's ordeal. "I never had any idea about the difficult road that she had been down, because she never let that show. Now I marvel at that," Cathy said. "And I have so much compassion for her and for other women—and men—who have gone through all of that."

Cathy received effective, coordinated care, full of hugs and genuine concern. "And it probably wasn't that way when Mary Jo went through it," she said. "I think that was part of her decision to get involved."

Occasionally Mary Jo's name comes up in conversations with patients at the Cropper Center, said Tina German, nurse navigator. "They'll say, 'Who was Mary Jo Cropper?' And I'll say, 'She's our namesake, and yes, she did lose her fight with breast cancer, but she didn't let it get her down.'"

Tina says she sees quite a few success stories but also has seen tragic endings. "When someone has a terminal diagnosis, it's so hard. Life's not fair," Tina said. "And sometimes, it just really sucks. You have to know the person well enough to know what to say."

Some patients eventually choose to stop treatments, as Mary Jo did. Yet researchers are coming up with new drugs all the time, Tina said, often giving hope where little or none had existed.

People often wonder why breast tissue seems vulnerable to cancer. Part of the answer, Tina said, is that "breast cancers are hormonally fed," and, because of hormones, breast tissues go through many changes.

As Billie Burrus, imaging navigator, puts it: "The number-one risk factor is that God gave you breasts and you're a woman. Number two is age." She likes to point out that because men are far less likely to get breast cancer, they typically have *no* information about the disease. So, staff members devote extra time to educating men who do receive a malignancy diagnosis.

In 2018, almost three hundred breast cancer cases were diagnosed at the Cropper Center—and none of those involved males. In fact, in her two decades of experience with breast patients, nurse Tina German has seen only four male breast cancer patients.

One of those was Steve Del Gardo.

A patient of the Cropper Center and a 2019 Angel award recipient, Steve approaches the disease with a unique blend of humor and serious concern. Steve jokes that he is among the 1 percent of men who are "lucky" enough to be diagnosed with breast cancer.

Steve, who lives in Taylor Mill, Kentucky, never got to meet Mary Jo because his cancer episode began more than a year after her death. In 2012, a lump in his chest kept growing larger and more painful, so his primary-care doctor sent him to the Cropper Center for testing.

"I saw a lot of women going into the building and I saw the sign had the word, 'breast,' in it, and I thought, 'I don't have *breasts*. I must be at the wrong place,'" he said. So Steve called his doctor, who said, no, he was exactly where he was supposed to be.

Once inside, Steve was handed some standard forms that every patient must fill out. Quite a few of the questions didn't really apply to him; here are two examples of those—with his humorous responses.

How many pregnancies have you had? "One. I have a son."

When was your last menstrual period? "Never. But I do get grumpy as hell every three weeks."

On a serious note, Steve said the female-oriented content of those forms underscores the fact that people *assume* breast cancer afflicts women only. Filling out the patient-intake forms was the first of many awkward moments Steve experienced as a male with the disease. He was diagnosed with Stage II breast cancer. "That was scary enough. But what I was told afterward was scarier," Steve said. "The doctor told me, 'If you had waited another month or two, I'd be telling you to get your life in order.'"

The next hour was a blur. Steve dissolved into tears and confusion. "I didn't even know that men could *get* breast cancer," Steve said. "It was hard to comprehend."

Next, he had a double mastectomy. And four rounds of chemo. Steve jokes about the warnings he received about the side effects: "So my hair will come back blacker and thicker? I'll lose weight? And this will kill the cancer? Sounds like three great benefits of this chemotherapy stuff!" Kidding aside, chemotherapy and preventative medications did come with horrible side effects, especially nausea, Steve said.

In 2013, Steve was at his parents' house in Loveland, Ohio, recovering from a second round of chemo, "and a warm sensation came over my body," Steve said. "A bright light came into the room and I heard a voice that said, 'Start a foundation to help men.'" Steve questioned whether his medications were making him hallucinate. But he also thought perhaps the idea was divine inspiration. So, he started Protect the Pecs, a male breast cancer foundation; it helps men who are in need of support, provides funds for research and cultivates public awareness.

Steve has done quite a few public presentations on behalf of Protect the Pecs.

Steve said he appreciated seeing his efforts recognized, which brings more awareness to his cause. He also is grateful for the care that the Cropper Center staff extended to him. "They treat you like family. They make you feel welcome, and it's not a scary place, like some doctors' offices," Steve said.

He advises anyone with cancer: "Don't let it define you—and give back to the community when you can."

Steve, who used to work as a computer sales vice president, used his cancer as a wake-up call to fulfill a dream. Proud of his New York Italian heritage and family recipes for cannoli desserts, Steve started his own business, Del Gardo's, a cannoli shop and cafe in Covington, Kentucky.

Now known as "The Cannoli Guy," Steve still finds time to advocate for men with breast cancer, saying, "We're still many, many years away from society accepting the fact that men get breast cancer."

Using a picture of boxing gloves as a backdrop, Steve has used this slogan, which he says applies to anyone with cancer: "Instead of lying face-down in the fight against cancer, come out swinging and beat it down! Battle it with all of your strength, positivity, faith and humor! You will win!"

Even though Mary Jo ultimately lost her battle, her family believes she would not have survived as long without "her love of family, faith, friends, and the spirit to love life with a smile, through all adversity," her obituary said.

Mary Jo's making-memories mission had outlasted some predictions—and was more successful than she realized. And perhaps it was accomplished differently than she imagined. Because while her family and friends are glad that they were able to visit marvelous destinations with her, many of her loved ones hold more tightly to the everyday things she said, did and liked.

For them, each reminder of Mary Jo somehow feels more precious now than it did during her lifetime. A handwritten note on a plain piece of paper can be more treasured than a $500 David Yurman cable bracelet; a swig of Budweiser beer can seem as satisfying as a sip of Rombauer wine. These were among Mary Jo's favorite things, shared with some of her favorite people. They may hold no special significance to anyone else. But to those who loved her and miss her every day, they are, in fact, priceless.

As anyone who has ever lost a loved one knows, the hurt becomes less acute as time passes. Bitter pangs of grief subside into dull aches. And pleasant memories more readily inspire smiles.

But anytime a small reminder pops up, it's capable of triggering laughter, tears or just a deep sense of wistfulness. Mary Jo's family, friends and acquaintances will never stop longing for the piece that went missing from each heart she touched.

One unexpected reminder for Mary Jo's daughter, Amy, came in late 2019 with the release of a new movie, *Little Women*, based on the classic novel, by Louisa May Alcott. It's a story about four sisters making their own mark on the world, and Mary Jo loved the sisterhood that book explored, perhaps reminding her of her own upbringing with two sisters, Amy said. She imagined her mom would have loved seeing the motion picture adaptation.

Another example: When White Castle announced that beer would be served at some of its restaurants, Mary Jo's sister-in-law, Ginny Kuntz, kept thinking what a kick Mary Jo would have gotten out of enjoying a cold brew and hot sliders at the same time. Ginny lamented: "Oh, why aren't you *here*, Mary Jo?"

Each year, Ginny creates a Christmas display of items that Santa might have delivered: A Raggedy Ann doll, a little bear, some doll babies and a book that Mary Jo used to read aloud to her students: *Love You Forever* by Robert Munsch (Firefly Books, 1986). The book is about the relationship between a young mother and her child, as he grows up and she grows old. Reading that book always makes Ginny think of Mary Jo—and it invariably makes her cry. Ginny gave copies of the book to some of Mary Jo's closest friends after her memorial service.

Mary Jo's grandchildren cherish the love letters and journals she left behind. Amy's son, Drew, keeps his letter from her in a desk drawer at his father's house. "It's special to me," he said. "I like the part where she said it make her feel good when I would hug her and say, 'I love you, Mimi.'" Drew, who was not quite 11 years old when Mary Jo died, continued playing basketball, as she predicted in that letter.

Mary Jo closed the letter by encouraging her grandson to make the most of his life.

I just want you to know how special you are, and to remember: You can do anything you set your mind to, Drew. Who knows, someday you may be President!

Drew laughed about that suggestion because he has zero interest in politics. However, his Mimi would be proud to know that Drew went on to study agricultural systems management at her alma mater, Ohio State.

Mary Jo's niece, Sylvia Norris, gets sentimental when she reads a note card from Auntie Mary, thanking her for being part of Amy's 1996 wedding. Mary Jo expressed hope that Sylvia and Amy could remain close as they got older; perhaps Sylvia could be like the sister that Amy never had. Sylvia said the card makes her think of the closeness between the two youngest Stolle sisters: her mom, Gail Norris, and Mary Jo. "It reminds me of how fortunate Mom and Auntie Mary were to have each other," Sylvia said, "and I feel she wanted Amy and I to have what Mom and she had." Sylvia and Amy have, in fact, been close.

Gail and Mary Jo enjoyed the kind of bond that defies verbal description, yet it could have been *felt* by anyone who saw them together. "Mom misses her so much—the golf teams they played on together, the vacations they took, the dinners and family get-togethers," Sylvia said. "She is just not the same person without Mary Jo."

Friend Marsha Falknor marvels at all the ways Mary Jo has continued to influence many lives, including hers. Besides being a patient at the Cropper Center, Marsha has become great friends with Amy and with many other people connected to Mary Jo. In 2017, Marsha, Ginny and four other women traveled to Napa Valley, California. In honor of Mary Jo, they visited the Rombauer winery. "We lifted our glasses and toasted Mary Jo, overlooking the view, and kept saying, 'She should be here,'" Ginny said.

At her home in Florida, friend Martie Mehallis keeps an array of Mary Jo photos on top of a bedroom dresser. "No one is allowed to touch them," Martie said. "I come in here and talk, laugh, and usually end up yelling at her as I pass by."

Brenda Bingham, the Lebanon Presbyterian Church secretary, keeps a picture of Mary Jo, tanned and smiling, wearing a Hawaiian lei made of white-and-magenta orchids, on the bulletin board above her desk. Like Martie, Brenda sometimes speaks as though Mary Jo never left. And, in many ways, she hasn't.

"She impressed each and every one of us in so many different ways—as a friend, as a mentor, as a woman," Brenda said. "She'll always be a part of me. Because I'm alive, she's alive in me—and I know she's alive in my heart."

In 2019, Mary Jo's relatives were deeply touched when they learned about a generous donation to the Center, made in memory of Judy Jackson, who was one of the original 2011 Mary Jo's Angels honorees.

Judy's husband, Cletis, requested that the amount remain confidential, but officials confirmed that his gift honoring Judy stood out among the largest donations that the Center received since it opened.

Judy did not die from breast cancer, although she had suffered with the disease in 2003, Cletis said. Judy, who had tirelessly worked to organize cancer fundraisers, died on November 30, 2018, at UC Health's West Chester Hospital. Over a two-year period, she had suffered a series of strokes, falls and bleeding in her brain, her husband said.

Cletis said he contributed to the Cropper Center to honor his wife because she believed in the work being done there—and because she was so "deeply impressed and humbled" to receive the Angel award. "She was being acknowledged for her true beliefs," her husband said.

Judy behaved a lot like Mary Jo. "Anytime she would learn someone had cancer, especially breast cancer, she would offer to help—to just be there, be a friend, relate her experiences," Cletis said about his wife. And like Mary Jo, Judy never sought recognition. "She was a person who never thought she would win anything or be noted for anything," her husband said. "Judy was a very kind person. She wasn't outgoing. But everybody liked her, and she liked everybody. She had deep feelings about things."

Judy was also familiar with several people who were connected to the Cropper Center. Dr. Ching Ho, the center's co-medical director when it opened, had performed Judy's surgery at Bethesda North six years before the Cropper Center opened.

One of Judy's can't-miss annual events was the Cincinnati walk coordinated by Susan G. Komen for the Cure. Over the years, Judy raised more than $150,000 for that organization, her husband said.

Even though Judy was an accomplished fundraiser, gathering money wasn't her main motivation, Cletis said, as exemplified by a situation that arose one year. On the day of the walk, the weather was rainy and unpleasant. Several women cited the foul weather as the reason they weren't coming. "They said, 'After all, you've already got the money.' And that didn't sit well with Judy," Cletis said. "Judy said those women didn't have a clue. They didn't understand. She didn't want them there for their money. She wanted them there to support her and all the other survivors with their *presence*."

He said Judy's top concern was: What could she do for others?

Cletis helped sponsor the Angels gala and golf outing, then decided he wanted to do more to support the Cropper Center in its new home at the Thomas Center. Cletis said his wife would be happy to know that her name will be associated with programs the Center offers to minimize patients' suffering and inconvenience.

Judy had lost her hair during the course of her treatment, Cletis said, so he knows she would be happy about the "cold-cap" program that the Angels gala has supported. Researchers discovered that cooling patients' scalps during chemotherapy restricts blood flow and prevents chemicals from zapping hair follicles. The result: patients keep more of their hair—and their self-esteem. Cathy Chasteen, Mary Jo's niece, went through the cold-cap program and preserved about 75 percent of her hair. The loss was hardly noticeable to others, so she could go about her daily business without everyone knowing she was a cancer patient. Her hair never came out in clumps, so she never had to wear a wig, like her aunt Mary Jo did.

The downside: the high-tech cap that keeps the head cool must be worn for several hours, which can cause headaches. And the program is expensive. It runs about $1,500 per patient. But the Cropper Center has covered those costs for many patients with funds from the gala. Patients used to go off-site for the cold-cap program. But it is now offered at the Thomas Center—which now is also home to the TriHealth Cancer Institute. The Cropper Center's cancer patients can now choose to get those services— and many others—without leaving the Thomas building.

As the Cropper Center moves into the future in the Thomas Center, "the program is going to continue to be a leader and grow," predicted John Prout, former TriHealth CEO. "It will have its own identity and its own focus."

Research involving Cropper Center patients will continue to play an increasingly important role. Whenever possible, patients who are diagnosed with cancer are offered the chance to participate in clinical trials, which study new drugs, different treatment methods or assess other factors, such as quality of life—or even how weight loss can affect cancer prevention or recurrence.

Yun Mi Kwon, clinical oncology manager for TriHealth's Hatton Research Institute, explained: "It is a common misconception that clinical trials are solely experimental. In reality, clinical trials are the standard of care for patients with a cancer diagnosis and some of the most effective and coordinated care happens within a clinical trial."

Some patients may not meet criteria for being enrolled; others may not want to spend the extra time and effort that are required. But many patients do appreciate the extra monitoring and other benefits of being enrolled in the trials. The patient might see improvement in his or her condition, too. Even if that doesn't happen, many people still like the idea of contributing to research that can help other patients later.

The best treatments are still being discovered—and they're becoming more personalized. Researchers now analyze the genetics of not only the patient but also the genetics of his or her tumor—and then drugs can specifically target that cancer's genes, proteins and tissues. While chemotherapy is like a bomb that indiscriminately damages healthy cells as well as cancerous ones, targeted drug therapy is more like a sniper: The drug "takes aim" at cancer cells, intending to kill them or to stop them in their tracks.

Promising strides also are being made with immunotherapy, "a drug that stimulates the patient's immune system to recognize the cancer cells as foreign and attack them," Yun Mi said.

Still, there are risks and side effects with both targeted and immunotherapy treatments, but they tend to be more favorable than with chemotherapy, Yun Mi said.

Despite the progress, many people wonder: Why haven't researchers been able to cure cancer? Yun Mi's answer: "Cancer is not a single disease but many complex diseases.... We are seeing treatments that work initially, but after a period of time, the cancer 'learns' to adapt and evolve, finding ways to build up resistance and essentially 'outsmart' the treatment," she said. "We don't have all the answers, but some of the best treatment options for patients with cancer exist within a clinical trial. Cancer is something that has touched everyone, and the race to finding a cure continues."

Cancer has devastated countless families. In that regard, the Stolle-Cropper family has plenty of company.

That family, however, stands out for its extraordinary commitment to helping others—and not just financially, said former TriHealth CEO John Prout. The family works behind-the-scenes to plan the annual gala and finds other ways to help in creative ways, as Mary Jo did.

Prout said that, in his three decades of healthcare experience, "I have never seen such involvement from the family of a donor. The whole thing has been exciting and clearly a continuation of Mary Jo's legacy."

He said the Stolle-Cropper family has built a partnership with TriHealth, "and they have confidence they're getting a return for their money, their time and their emotional investment."

The family's commitment is something that new employees learn about from Billie Burrus, imaging navigator. With new hires, Billie routinely recounts a brief history of the Cropper Center, Mary Jo and her family. She also sometimes shares the story with patients. That's because it's important for people to know the ingredients that combined to make the Cropper Center a beautiful, comfortable place that provides high-quality, efficient service, Billie said.

"In today's world, where we can see such negativity, it just is amazing to see the opposite—how kind the Cropper family has been to this Center and to the women who are being served here," Billie said. "Yes, the patients know Mary Jo Cropper is 'somebody,' because her name is out there. But to know her and to know the kindness that she and her family have given is just tremendous. I feel like the Cropper family's goal is to spread as much goodness and kindness as they can—and that's how Mary Jo would have wanted it."

Mary Jo's most fervent hope, her son, Spence said, was this: "That other people's stories don't have to end like hers did."

Jamie Easterling, the former radiology manager who worked on the Cropper Center, described its lasting impact: "It created a picture of hope."

"Someone once said, 'I can't promise you a miracle, but I can promise you a movement.' When a patient comes here, we can promise them good process, best practices, a good atmosphere, and we can promise them hope," Jamie said. "This disease is not a black-and-white science; we lose a lot of these battles ... but you can't just accept it and *not* fight it. Look at Mary Jo—even when she was defeated, look at what good came from it."

Jamie said he likes to remind colleagues: "Someone's going to walk into our hospital today—and not walk out. We, as Good Samaritans and healthcare providers, have to provide them hope. And the platform that Mary Jo has created was 'Let's build hope.'"

If a dollar value could be placed on all the little things Mary Jo Cropper did, her contributions may have rivaled—or exceeded—the fortune that her entrepreneurial father, Ralph J. Stolle, had amassed.

But there's no way to calculate the sum total of the love she poured into handwritten notes, cards and letters; into the hugs, the smiles, the anonymous gifts. There's no way to assess how much she enriched the lives of family, friends, students, neighbors, dozens of cancer patients and thousands of healthy people who just need annual screenings.

So even without her big gift to the Center, Mary Jo had lived a life of significance; she took meaningful action, scattering points of light that keep her memory burning brightly.

Mary Jo's loved ones hope that you, the person reading her story, will be inspired to take your own action.

Maybe you'll decide to fearlessly discuss cancer, whether you have it or not, instead of avoiding the subject.

Maybe you'll write a good, old-fashioned note to brighten someone's day, especially if that someone has cancer.

Maybe you'll give one dollar—or one million dollars—to fight against the disease.

Somehow, you can find a way to be like Mary Jo—and like the Center named for her.

You, too, can become A Comforting Light.

Author's Note

Before I was asked to write this book in 2019, I was a news reporter for almost three decades, mostly covering crime. In fact, my first book, released in 2018, focused on a controversial court case. But during my journalism career, I had often delved into people's life histories for personality profiles and for obituaries—and I always loved digging for the special nuggets that make each person unique. So, when Cathy Chasteen, Mary Jo Stolle Cropper's niece, approached me about writing this book, I knew that I would enjoy learning about Mary Jo's life. I had already written stories about her family for *The Cincinnati Enquirer* in years past. And I was familiar with the mark that the Stolle name had made on Warren County, Ohio, where I live.

This opportunity intrigued me. And I felt honored that Mary Jo's loved ones had chosen me to tell her story. But I felt a slight hesitancy—because much of her story revolved around C-A-N-C-E-R. That was something I knew very little about and, frankly, was almost afraid to learn about. I noticed my own repulsion as I repeatedly heard that word—and typed it, researched it, contemplated it, discussed it.

Lots of people feel that way. And I, like most people, had repressed those feelings. Many people don't want to admit how disquieting that word can be. It's as if we subconsciously fear that talking about cancer lends more power to it. Or maybe, if we mistakenly utter it too many times, we might conjure it up like the menacing spirit in the movie, *Beetlejuice*.

After much personal reflection, I have concluded that the opposite is true. Talking about—and writing about—cancer in an upfront, honest way is important, even if it's not pleasant. Because, in doing so, we respect those who have been afflicted with it. We validate people whose loved ones have suffered with it. We enlighten people who haven't had cancer and hope to God that they never do. We honor the memory of those who succumbed to it, such as Mary Jo. And we inspire people to contribute to its eradication.

While writing about Mary Jo's final days, I caught myself wishing that I were a fiction writer, just this once. That way, I could use the magic of my keystrokes to keep my protagonist alive. The heroine of this story deserved that.

Writing the chapters about her death and funeral hurt. I had absorbed such emotional impact from everyone I've interviewed, I was almost paralyzed. Yet I know that I still cannot fully understand what Mary Jo—and all who loved her—endured. Nor do I pretend to understand what other cancer patients go through.

At the same time, I realized that cancer isn't really the star of this show. Mary Jo is. Because this is truly a story about the tremendous impact of one life, well-lived. It's a story that underscores the importance of little things that don't cost a cent, even though it's also a story about a million-dollar donation and its huge multiplier effect.

Although the ending isn't the one that any of us would have preferred, Mary Jo's loved ones hope that telling her story will encourage many other "Mary Jos," whether or not they are afflicted with cancer or blessed with wealth.

It's a story that never would have been told if not for the love, strength and commitment of dozens of people who cared enough to contribute to this work—and it wasn't easy for any of them. It's one thing to reveal thoughts off the top of your head. It's another to extract old, buried memories and feelings that dwell inside your heart, then entrust those to someone you barely know: me, the writer.

Those were the types of interviews that friends and relatives of Mary Jo Cropper shared with me to make this book possible. We laughed, cried and spent hours poring over old records and photos to achieve one goal: to convey the essence of who Mary Jo was, so that readers of her story would be informed, touched and changed by it in positive ways. That was the effect it had on me as I researched it and wrote it.

I developed tremendous respect and affection for each person who subjected themselves to my incessant questioning. Mary Jo surely would have been proud of them, even if she would've disliked having so many people focused on her so intently, prodded by a dogged old newshound.

Together, we worked to expand the palette used to "paint" Mary Jo's life portrait—many bright, joyous swaths interspersed with patches of darkness; sometimes in broad brushstrokes, sometimes with finely detailed ones. Dozens of people stepped up to the canvas and made splashes, big and small. I just decided how to arrange those contributions into the most authentic portrayal possible.

It is my hope that the portrait that unfolded in the preceding pages is vivid, insightful and inspiring to all who view it. And most of all, I hope it comes close to being as beautiful as Mary Jo was, inside and out.

To contact Janice, or to obtain more information, please visit janicehisle.com.

Acknowledgments

Mary Jo's niece, **Cathy Chasteen**, was the driving force behind this book. I was flattered when Cathy informed me that she had read some of my writing and wanted me to tell the story of her dear aunt, Mary Jo Cropper, and the Center she helped establish.

I have often told her: "Every family should have a Cathy." But few families are blessed with a person who cares so deeply about family history. Cathy has made significant emotional and financial investments to reveal, preserve and share her dearest relatives' life stories. Besides working with me on this book, Cathy worked with another writer, Geoffrey Williams, on the book about her grandfather, *Ingenuity in a Can: The Ralph Stolle Story* (Orange Frazer Press, 2004).

While Cathy and I worked on *A Comforting Light*, she fielded torrents of text messages from me. She deftly navigated sensitive issues and removed roadblocks from my path. And, incredibly, Cathy undertook this endeavor in mid-2019 just after finishing chemotherapy for her own breast cancer, which was diagnosed in late 2018. She was still undergoing some treatments as of early 2020, when this book was completed.

Cathy said it became clear to her that her aunt's story was worthy of a book after her own cancer gave her a small sample of what Mary Jo endured. "I was mortified about everything she had to go through, and I thought people should know about that—and about her," Cathy said.

Cathy is one of the most thoughtful, patient and empathetic people I've ever met. I am privileged to now count her—and others I met throughout this project—among my friends.

My heartfelt appreciation and earnest respect are extended to Cathy and to all of her relatives—the entire Stolle-Cropper family—for the kindness they showed me as a person and for their patience with me as a researcher and writer, hell-bent on pinning down the smallest details.

I heartily thank Mary Jo's relatives who withstood the most rigorous questioning I could dish out: her son, **Spencer Cropper**, and his wife, **Dana Cropper**; Mary Jo's daughter, **Amy Cropper Winkler**; and sister-in-law, **Ginny Kuntz**. Their interviews, along with those from Mary Jo's niece, Cathy Chasteen, formed the foundation of this book.

Mary Jo's sisters were also incredibly willing to help. The sister who was emotionally closest to Mary Jo, **Gail Stolle Norris**, was among the people who continued to hurt most deeply over the loss of Mary Jo. Gail pushed through emotions that remained raw despite the passage of time; her daughter, **Sylvia Norris**, helped ease that process for Gail and for me. I thank both of them. I also am grateful to Mary Jo's oldest sister, **Sandy Stolle Perry**. She shared decades-old recollections with amazing accuracy, often injecting a witty remark or a bit of dry humor. Thank you for keeping me on my toes, and for sharing more than a few laughs between the sentimental moments, Sandy.

Other major building blocks of this book came from the Stolle-Cropper family's "extended family" at Bethesda North Hospital and at the Mary Jo Cropper Family Center for Breast Care. Without a doubt, the person who fielded the most questions from me in that group was the Bethesda Foundation's **Mary Fischer**.

She is owed a heaping shovelful of gratitude. I have joked that my approach to journalism—and to book-writing—was inspired by the detective from the classic TV show, *Columbo*. His signature gimmick: As Columbo would exit a room, he would typically turn around and ask "just one more thing...." I used that line on Mary Fischer more times than she probably cares to recount. Mary responded quickly and courteously to dozens of my requests. This book probably would not have been possible without her.

I am grateful to **Dr. Susan Weinberg** for carving out time for interviews, reading chapters, fact-checking and producing the

Foreword. Her former administrative assistant, **Regina Eaton**, is to be commended for the articulate and heartfelt interview she gave, and for unearthing the eulogy that Susan read at Mary Jo's funeral. **Tina German**, nurse navigator, gave me a tour and interview that were essential to my understanding of the Cropper Center and how it functions, as was my interview with **Billie Burrus**, imaging navigator. Tina and Billie are two of the best ambassadors that the Cropper Center could ever hope to have. Both were candid, articulate and personable.

Another person who deserves recognition is TriHealth Breast Program Manager **Jacqui Appel**, who helped fill in many gaps. Jacqui impressed me with her charming personality and her absolute devotion to her work. Imaging supervisor **Don Owens**, former Bethesda surgeon **Dr. Ted Jones** and clinical oncology research manager **Yun Mi Kwon** also dedicated time to helping me understand their work.

Two of the most articulate hospital executives I could ever imagine, **John Prout** and **Jamie Easterling**, dispensed with corporate jargon and spoke from the heart.

Interviews with Mary Jo's friends cemented together all the other materials that make up this book. **Martie Mehallis, Nancy Sholder** and **Marsha Falknor** were among those who provided the most heartfelt and vivid recollections. Key additional information came from **Talitha Colston, Bill Falknor, Marilyn Keever Long, Pam Hatfield Russell, Joan Zecher** and **Dick Zecher**.

Sally Alspaugh Finn, chartered advisor in philanthropy, gave the "inside story" of seminal events in the Cropper Center's creation—and she played a pivotal role in the creation of this book. Sally has an incredible talent for connecting people who can help each other. She was the one who connected Mary Jo to the Bethesda Foundation, leading to Mary Jo's million-dollar gift. And Sally was also the person who read my first book then connected me with Cathy Chasteen when she was in search of an author. Without Sally's involvement, I almost certainly would not have been involved in this process. Thank you, Sally, for believing in my abilities, and for setting up one of the most rewarding experiences of my life.

I also am grateful to **Steve Del Gardo**. He candidly shared his unusual perspective as a male with breast cancer. I intended only to do a short phone interview with him. But his personality was so intoxicating, my husband and I made a special point of meeting with Steve in person at his successful cannoli business in Covington, Kentucky. Steve has my heartfelt thanks and sincere wishes for continued good health.

Cletis Jackson, who made a large contribution to the Center in memory of his deceased wife, Judy, trusted me with his emotional story even though I was a total stranger to him. Thank you, Cletis.

Behind the scenes, my husband, **Michael Hisle**, devoted countless hours to this work. He counseled me as I pondered how to handle sensitive situations. He read rough drafts at all hours of the day and night. He lovingly prepared meals and brought them to me while I was chained to my computer, writing feverishly. He kissed away my tears and, as always, cheered me on when I doubted myself. I honor and thank you, dearest Michael. Every good thing I have accomplished during the past fourteen years would have been impossible if not for you.

Additional encouragement and advice came from my sister, **Sandy Peate**; and from my dear friends **Sharlene Chapman**, **Debbie Silverman** and **Terri Curnayn**; and from fellow authors **Diana Bosse** and **Peter Bronson**.

I am grateful to proofreader **Jane Wenning** for her eagle eye, and to **Orange Frazer Press** for presenting these words so beautifully.

THANK YOU to every person who contributed to this book in any way, whether mentioned explicitly here or not.

Above all, thank you, **Mary Jo Stolle Cropper**, for living such an extraordinary life and for leaving such a noteworthy legacy.

The limitations of the written word render us unable to look into Mary Jo's eyes, to hear her voice or to feel her life's energy. But she did build so much during her life, most notably brighter futures for everyone she served: students, relatives, friends, strangers.

If we pay close attention to all of that, and to the words in this book, we cannot help but feel her presence. We cannot help but feel hope.

References

To authenticate and supplement interviews, the author obtained numerous documents from interviewees. Direct quotes and paraphrases from those materials helped form the narrative of this book. In addition, the author verified events and other historical facts via multiple internet sites and relied upon records from the following sources:

· The Bethesda Foundation—fundraising facts and history of the breast center at Bethesda North Hospital, along with scripts of Grand Opening speeches
· Centerville City Schools, Centerville, Ohio—Mary Jo Cropper's employment records
· The Commonwealth of Kentucky Registrar of Vital Statistics—Stolle family death certificates
· The Department Store Museum, www.thedepartmentstoremuseum.org—descriptions of Rike's department store, provided in photos and written materials
· Lebanon City Schools, Lebanon, Ohio—Mary Jo Cropper's high school yearbook and employment records
· The National Cancer Institute—statistical data and other information about cancer
· Ohio Department of Education—Mary Jo Cropper's employment history
· Ohio Department of Health/Vital Statistics—Stolle and Cropper family death certificates
· Ohio Secretary of State—Ralph Stolle business records
· The Ohio State University—information about Stolle and Cropper family scholarships

- Warren County (Ohio) Probate Court—Cropper and Stolle family marriage, divorce and estate records
- Wright State University's special collection—Rike's department store history

Additional information, photographs and/or permissions were provided by: Andy Swallow of the Bethesda Foundation; photographers D.A. Fleischer and a niece of Mary Jo Cropper, Kris Marr; Centerville City Schools; Nancy Sholder and the Lebanon Presbyterian Church Cancer Support Group; Warren County Engineer Neil Tunison and staff; staff of the Warren County Health Department; John Zimkus, Warren County Historical Society, Lebanon, Ohio; Patricia Haynes, Cindi West and Todd Yohey of Lebanon City Schools; a dear friend of the author, Katie Eastman; The Ohio State University, Columbus, Ohio; Mike Samet, spokesman for Hamilton County Public Health, Cincinnati, Ohio.

Mary Jo's Angels Honorees

2011
Darlene Greene/Emily's Beads of Courage
Judy Jackson
Betty Powley
Nancy Sholder
Sand Dollar Sisters

2012
Mindy Atwood/Patches of Light
Tom & Bonnie Collins
Judy Conrad
Ed Hartman
Miriam McAllister

2013
Lessie Bidermann & Connie Ward
Ria Davidson/The Dragonfly Foundation
Lisa Farrell & Camie Cusick/The Karen Wellington Foundation
Molly Hodapp
Sue Tollefson

2014
Amy Pritchard
Harold Thomas
Talika Dennis-Carter
Mike Shroder & Patty Stump
Lynn Pierce/Josh Cares organization

2015
Anne Abate
Dr. Kimberly Koss
Kathy Leurck & Zand Walters/The Karen Wellington Foundation
Jon Jamison, Hope Jamison and Cheryl Saylor/Jaymie Jamison Foundation for Hope

2016
Traci Martin
Rowin Floth
Josephine Holloman-Adams
Rebecca Bradley
Cathy Halloran

2017
Elaine Mahaffey
Traci Clancy

2018
Anna Frank
Kelli Kolkmeyer

2019
Kent Wellington/The Karen Wellington Foundation
Steve Del Gardo
Alana Ralph & Allie Steiner

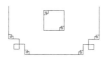

A Comforting Recipe: Dorothy Stolle's Sour Cream Coffeecake

As shared by her daughter, Mary Jo Stolle Cropper

1 c. margarine	1 c. sour cream
2 eggs	1 t. baking powder
2 c. sifted Swans Down Cake Flour	¼ t. salt
2 c. sugar	1½ t. vanilla extract

· Cream together margarine, sugar, eggs. Fold in sour cream and vanilla carefully. Sift together dry ingredients and add to mixture.
· Spoon half the batter into a greased and floured 10-inch tube pan. Cover with half of topping and repeat.

Topping
½ c. finely chopped pecans
½ t. cinnamon
2 T. brown sugar

· Mix together well.
· Bake in a 350-degree oven for 50–60 minutes. Cool almost completely before removing from pan. Sprinkle with confectioner's sugar on top. Serve cold.

Each time you prepare this recipe, we know that you will think of Mary Jo and her family.
We also hope you will ask yourself: What can I do to comfort or help someone today?

Index